AFC WIMBLEDON
A PICTORIAL HISTORY

GRAHAM MOODY

AMBERLEY

ACKNOWLEDGEMENTS

Thank you to photographer Paul Willatts, who provided a lot of the pictures in the book, and also to Newsquest, the owners of the *Wimbledon Guardian* newspaper, for permission to use the pictures taken for them by DeadlinePix photo agency. They took some fantastic pictures, without which the book would not have been possible. I would also like to mention all those who wrote match and news reports for the AFC Wimbledon club website and the *Wimbledon Guardian* website. Both sites provided an invaluable source of material, as did the Football Club History Database and Niall Couper's *This Is Our Time* book.

Dedicated to my family and my gorgeous Alana.
And to my grandad. You always believed in me and this book is for you.

Front cover: Danny Kedwell celebrates his promotion-winning penalty in the Conference play-off final, May 2011. (Paul Willatts)

First published 2013

Amberley Publishing
The Hill, Stroud
Gloucestershire, GL5 4EP

www.amberleybooks.com

Copyright © Graham Moody, 2013

The right of Graham Moody to be identified as the Author
of this work has been asserted in accordance with the
Copyrights, Designs and Patents Act 1988.

All rights reserved. No part of this book may be reprinted or reproduced or utilised in any form or by any electronic, mechanical or other means, now known or hereafter invented, including photocopying and recording, or in any information storage or retrieval system, without the permission in writing from the Publishers.

British Library Cataloguing in Publication Data.
A catalogue record for this book is available from the British Library.

ISBN 978 1 4456 1357 4 (print)
ISBN 978 1 4456 1364 2 (ebook)

Typesetting and Origination by Amberley Publishing.
Printed in the UK.

INTRODUCTION

This book is a journey through the remarkable history of AFC Wimbledon and its supporters. In just eleven seasons, they experienced all the highs and lows of England's national game, from seeing their club ripped away from them, to starting again and rising through the non-League ranks to reclaim their rightful place in the Football League.

For every championship title, play-off thriller and cup success, there was disappointment, fights with the authorities and emotional goodbyes.

This book aims to capture all of that, and show just how the supporters of one club picked themselves off the ground in 2002 to come back bigger and stronger against all the odds – even if nobody wanted them to. It is a club all about those supporters, many of whom work for free around the stadium and never grumble about it, happy enough just to have a club to support. It is a football club run by football fans, for football fans.

I was lucky enough to get the job of AFC Wimbledon reporter when I joined the *Wimbledon Guardian* sports desk in February 2011. I had been at other papers around the newspaper group for four years, but adding Wimbledon coverage to my working week turned into a delight. The club and the people in it were always welcoming, understanding and willing to help – something you don't always get in football. It made me understand almost straight away why the Dons are such a special club.

I spent eighteen months reporting on Wimbledon, and I am proud to say I was at the City of Manchester Stadium that day in May. Nine years of hard work culminated in that Seb Brown penalty save and that Danny Kedwell spot-kick that put them back among the big boys of the Football League – the prize they had wanted from the start. The emotion and joy that emanated from the club and its supporters that day is something I will never forget. They had been told their team would not be in the wider interests of football, but they had proven everyone wrong.

When the chance arose for me to write this book, I jumped at it. I have enjoyed writing it and it has been a journey for me too. If anything, I have fallen in love with the club all over again.

The main aim is to give a brief history of how the Dons got from that unbelievable day in 2002 back to the Football League, and how, once they got there, they had to fight to stay. Alongside the history and the words, there are some splendid pictures of all the big moments. Many of them will not have seen before but some are no doubt replicated on the walls of Wimbledon fans throughout the south London town.

I hope you enjoy reading this as much as I have enjoyed writing it.

Seb Brown keeps goal in front of a stand full of AFC Wimbledon fans during the Conference play-off final at the City of Manchester stadium in 2011. (Newsquest)

1

NOT IN THE WIDER INTERESTS OF FOOTBALL

28 May 2002: a day that changed the lives of Wimbledon Football Club fans everywhere. It was the day a three-man panel set up by the Football Association ratified a wealthy businessman's previously absurd-sounding plan to take Wimbledon Football Club out of south London and move it 56 miles north to the new city of Milton Keynes. It was also the day AFC Wimbledon was born.

Started by Ivor Heller, Trevor Williams, Marc Jones and Kris Stewart, the club made a laughing stock of the FA's decision and the panel's report that said a new club, set up by fans, 'Would not be in the wider interests of football.' It was not the first time Wimbledon as a club had faced adversity and come out the other side the better for it.

Formed in 1889, Wimbledon first existed as Wimbledon Old Centrals, a team that played on Wimbledon Common, established by ex-pupils of Old Central School. Despite success in the amateur south London and Surrey leagues and cups, their struggles for a permanent home saw them shut down in 1910. That could have been a very early end for Wimbledon but, two years later, they were back in another guise. Junior sides Wimbledon Corporation Employees and Wimbledon St Andrews merged to form Wimbledon Borough, with the help of former Wimbledon players. They played in the Suburban League and soon Borough was dropped from the name to leave it as just Wimbledon FC – a name that would last for ninety-two years. A year later they had a permanent home too, when they bought an area of disused swampland at the corner of Haydon's Road and Plough Lane in Merton. It was to be their home for the next seventy-nine years.

Over the next seven decades, they made their mark in non-League football. In 1921, they moved to the top amateur league in the country, the Isthmian League, and won it three times in the lead up to the Second World War. They also won the Surrey Charity Shield four times, the London Senior Cup, the Surrey Combination Cup, the South Western Junior Cup and the South London Charity Cup.

After a period of decline, chairman Sydney Black brought in Les Henley as coach in 1955, and he reversed the club's fortunes. They won the Isthmian League again in 1959, and then for three seasons in a row from 1962. Having been losing finalists twice in the FA Amateur Cup (in 1935 when they lost 2-1 in a replay to Bishop Auckland and in 1947 when they lost 2-1 to Leytonstone), it was third time lucky in 1963 when four headed Eddie Reynold's goals gave them a 4-2 win over Sutton United at Wembley.

The next step was to turn professional, which they did in 1964, by moving to the Southern League First Division. They won promotion to the Premier Division in their first season and won their first professional trophy in 1970 when they won the Southern League Cup. Although everything may have seemed rosy, it wasn't, and financial troubles meant the club needed a £2,500 donation from the Supporters' Club in May 1974 to keep them alive – not the last time the fans would come to the club's rescue.

The introduction of Allen Batsford that same year instigated Wimbledon's climb up the leagues. He led them to three Southern League titles in a row, and they became the first non-League side to win at a top-flight team in the FA Cup, when they beat Burnley 1-0 at Turf Moor with a Mick Mahon goal. They held Leeds to a 0-0 draw in the fourth round thanks to Dickie Guy's penalty save at Elland Road, before Dave Bassett's own goal meant a 1-0 replay defeat. Just thirteen years later they would be lifting the trophy.

Despite their league success, election to the Football League was not automatic, and instead clubs had to be voted in. After two seasons of missing out, businessman Ron Noades was brought in as owner in 1977, and he politicised the fans into a campaign that pressurised the Football League and finally earned Wimbledon their place among the big boys.

A bad start saw Batsford replaced by Dario Gradi midway through the first season, and over the next five years the Dons yo-yoed between the Fourth and Third Divisions as off-field problems persisted. Rumours circulated Noades was to take the club north when he bought Milton Keynes City for £1, but nothing happened and, instead, Noades bought Crystal Palace and sparked talks of a merger. The same supporters Noades had politicised to get the club into the Football League took up their protest banners again, and convinced the Football League to introduce rules preventing people owning more than one club. Noades chose Palace over Wimbledon and took Gradi with him. Sam Hammam became the Dons' majority shareholder, with Bassett as manager.

Under Bassett they won the Fourth Division in 1983, were promoted from the Third Division as runners-up in 1984 and, in 1986, secured their place in the First Division for the very first time. It had only been nine years since they entered the Football League.

They defied critics to briefly top the league in their first season, before going on to finish sixth as Bassett quit for Watford after falling out with Hammam. Bobby Gould took charge and led Wimbledon to their most memorable success. Having beaten Luton Town 2-1 in the 1988 FA Cup semi-finals, no one gave the Dons a chance in the final at Wembley against Liverpool. But they defied all odds, and Lawrie Sanchez's header and Dave Beasant's penalty save gave them a shock 1-0 win. Commentator John Motson coined the name that became synonymous with the club when he said, 'The Crazy Gang has beaten the Culture Club.' The Dons were only the second team to win both the FA Amateur Cup and the FA Cup, ninety-four years after Old Carthusians had become the first.

Wimbledon established themselves as a top-flight side, but problems mounted behind the scenes. Plough Lane needed redeveloping due to the Taylor Report demanding that top-tier sides had all-seater stadiums, but Hammam's attempts were blocked by a clause that let Merton Council have the stadium for £8,000 if the club went into liquidation. The cost of removing the clause proved too much and, on the last day of the 1990/91 season, Hammam announced that the Dons were leaving Plough Lane to groundshare with Palace. It was the beginning of the end for Wimbledon.

When Hammam persuaded two Norwegian businessmen, Kjell Inge Rokke and Bjorn Rune Gjelston, to invest about £28 million in the club for an 80 per cent stake, it brought about plans to move to Dublin in Ireland. Once more, Dons fans protested, and the plans were shelved when the Football Association of Ireland opposed the move and proposals to build a casino on the proposed new stadium site were rejected.

When manager Joe Kinnear suffered a heart attack during a game in March 1999 and was replaced by Norwegian Egil Olsen, the Dons began losing their Crazy Gang identity. They also lost their Premier League status for the first time in fourteen years in 2000, and Olsen was replaced by Terry Burton with three games to go.

Hammam sold his remaining interest in the club and South African Charles Koppel was installed as chairman by the Norwegian owners. It was under him that in the summer of 2001 the controversial move to Milton Keynes began. Milton Keynes mogul Peter Winkelman had begun to appear around Selhurst Park and, on 2 August, fans received a letter from Koppel detailing his plans. The Dons' fans immediately went into action and Stewart, chair of the Wimbledon Independent Supporters' Association (WISA), organised protests and campaigns that included a release of black balloons in the first League game against Birmingham and a boycott of season tickets for the 2002/03 season. Supporters Direct, an organisation set up to help fans have a bigger say in the world of football, advised Wimbledon's supporters to set up a supporters' trust, which resulted in the first meeting of the Dons Trust at Wimbledon Community Centre on 25 October 2001. It gathered pace quickly, and more than 1,200 fans attended the official launch at New Wimbledon Theatre. Stewart chaired the meeting, with Allen Batsford and Dickie Guy among the speakers, and there was a parade of former players.

When the Football League board voted unanimously against the move, it should have been the end of the matter, but Koppel pledged to continue his battle and even threatened the club with liquidation if the move did not happen. He managed to force an appeal against the board's decision and then the real battle started.

The Football Association set up a three-man commission to consider the case at its headquarters in Soho Square, London. It began on 14 May and comprised Isthmian League chairman and FA representative Alan Turvey, Aston Villa secretary Steve Stride and media lawyer Raj Parker, with Wimbledon fans standing vigil outside the building.

Both sides presented their arguments to the panel, but although many believed the ruling would come down in favour of the supporters, it did not. A 2-1 vote in favour of the move left the football world startled. It was crushing for Dons fans, who stormed the Soho Square lobby and threw eggs at the building. They weren't to know it, but a miraculous story was beginning to brew.

Heller, a big Wimbledon fan, had been researching the possibility of a new club since November and met with fellow supporter Williams the morning of the decision. From that moment he decided his old club was dead and a new one was the only way forward. They were joined later by another Dons fan, Marc Jones, who also spoke at the Fox & Grapes pub in Wimbledon Village that night, where supporters had congregated to drown their sorrows, and WISA chairman Stewart, and the four began finding out what needed to be done. In short, they needed a league to play in, a groundshare agreement and to have been accepted into the London FA all in the space of a few weeks.

Wimbledon fans protest against the planned move to Milton Keynes during a game at Selhurst Park in 2001. (Paul Willatts)

An office was set up at Heller's factory and Stewart's impassioned speech at the WISA AGM on 30 May convinced the 1,000 supporters present that a new club was the best course of action. Isthmian League representatives were confident that the Dons would be voted into their league at their AGM, while forms were successfully completed for the London FA. That left the search for a ground, but that proved surprisingly easy. Plenty of clubs were willing to help out, but after rejecting offers from Dulwich and Leatherhead, Heller met with Kingstonian owner Rajesh Khosla and agreed a deal for the Dons to play at Kingsmeadow in Kingston. It wasn't Merton, but it was the closest option.

A Dons Trust meeting on 13 June saw the Trust take over AFC Wimbledon from Heller, Stewart and Williams, who had set it up in their own names, and announce the groundshare. Terry Eames, who had played for the club during the late 1970s and managed in the non-League, had been helping the Trust and was named manager. Erik Samuelson, a Sunderland fan converted to Wimbledon by his sons, was also brought onboard as finance director and would go on to be one of the club's most heroic figures.

It was all moving at an incredibly fast pace, but there was to be one huge setback. On 17 June, the Isthmian League held its AGM. Stewart and Heller waited patiently outside the meeting at the Le Meridien Hotel at Gatwick Airport, confident of success, but were left crestfallen. The motion needed 95 per cent of votes in favour, but it fell short with 87 per cent. It was a body blow, and those waiting in the Fox & Grapes to celebrate were shell-shocked. Two weeks of hard graft that had raised £75,000, a six-figure sponsorship deal with Sports Interactive Games, the creators of the Championship Manager computer game ... had all been for nothing.

In true Wimbledon fashion though, there was no giving up. That very same night, Combined Counties League secretary Alan Constable contacted Stewart and Heller, and the next day there was a meeting between the club and league. It was a step lower than Wimbledon would have liked, but it was a league to be play in. The league held its AGM on 24 June and, when it was proposed by Withdean 2000 FC and Hartley Wintney FC that the Dons join, it was approved by a majority – much to the relief of every Wimbledon fan.

The supporters had done it. A month after being told in the commission's report not to, they had set up their own club from scratch. AFC Wimbledon had a ground and a league to play in and were ready for action. It was a remarkable achievement.

The gathered crowd listen with interest to the ideas of the Dons Trust at its launch at New Wimbledon Theatre in February 2002. (Paul Willatts)

2

MAKING THEIR MARK

AFC Wimbledon's first season in the Combined Counties Premier League was far removed from anything their fans had experienced before or expected. They had to acclimatise to grounds that held 200 rather than 20,000, and spend more than their fair share of time in the mud and the rain watching Terry Eames' side challenge at the top, but eventually finish third. Considering where they had come from though, amassing more than 100 points in their debut season was still a success.

Their fortunes were going in the opposite direction to Wimbledon FC. They struggled for crowds at Selhurst Park, and even saw other club's supporters go to Kingsmeadow to watch AFC Wimbledon play rather than watch their own team when they played Wimbledon. At the end of the season, they upped sticks to the Milton Keynes National Hockey Stadium, and a year later renamed themselves MK Dons, having been bought out of administration by Peter Winkelman.

But AFC Wimbledon were leaving that team far behind. After being accepted in the Combined Counties, the first order of was to get a team together. On 30 June, they held open trials on Wimbledon Common and were inundated with around 300 potential footballers, far more than anticipated. It was down to Eames, with a little help from former Wimbledon manager Terry Burton, to decide who would and wouldn't be good enough as he whittled them down into a squad. He would go on to use fifty-two players in pre-season before settling on who would lead their promotion charge.

Their first friendly was at Sutton United on 10 July, just six weeks after the FA panel's decision. Fans flocked to the ground and the kick-off had to be delayed by thirty minutes to get the entire 4,656 crowd in. They watched a goalless first half, before Sutton scored four after the break – with future favourite Kevin Cooper scoring twice for United. The result didn't stop Wimbledon fans invading the pitch at full-time to celebrate the fact they had a club again. Of the eighteen players that played, only four would go on to be part of the squad for the opening day of the season – Sim Johnston, Glen Mulcaire, Dave Fry and Carlo Castronovo.

With Eames experimenting with players, pre-season results were not good, as the Dons lost their first nine before beating Enfield Town 3-2 for the Supporters Direct Cup in their final preparation match. Their first goal came from Mulcaire, when he scored a spectacular volley in their third friendly, a 2-1 defeat to Bromley. He made eight appearances for Wimbledon, but was soon making national headlines when named as the private investigator hired by newspapers to tap the phones of celebrities. In June 2007, he was jailed for six months after pleading guilty of illegally intercepting phone messages from Clarence House.

Simon Bassey began what was to be a long association with the club in the 5-0 defeat to Walton & Hersham, and Cooper arrived from Sutton in time for the 1-0 defeat at Windsor & Eton. Soon enough though, it was time for the Dons to play their first-ever competitive fixture.

On 17 August 2002, they travelled to Sandhurst Town for their Combined Counties League opener. Joe Sheerin captained the side in front of 2,249 supporters and Cooper and Keith Ward scored goals in the first half to secure a memorable 2-1 win. Plenty of celebrations that night saw management and players mingling with fans over a drink in the pub.

Four days after beating Sandhurst, the Dons had their first home match, against Chipstead. Celebrations were in full swing with 4,215 fans supporting the team and hundreds more left outside. Former Wimbledon players Jason Euell, Marcus Gayle and Neal Ardley all turned up, but Chipstead had not read the script, doing their best to spoil the party by winning 2-1.

The games came thick and fast, with two more in the next week that saw the Dons beat Cove at home 3-2 thanks to a late Lee Sidwell – brother to Premier League footballer Steve Sidwell – goal, and then lose 3-2 at one of the pre-season favourites, Ash United, where Cooper scored twice.

It was soon clear that the title would be a three-way fight between the Dons, the early pacesetters Wallingford, and Withdean 2000. But when it came to the crunch games, Wimbledon were not up to the task. They played Withdean in their seventh match, but came back from the South Coast with a 2-0 defeat having been largely outplayed.

They reacted by winning their next ten games. The run included coming back from 3-1 down to beat North Greenford United 4-3, scoring five goals in back-to-back games against Frimley Green and Bedfont, with Ally Russell scoring the club's first ever hat-trick in a 4-0 win over Cobham.

Trialists are put to the test on Wimbledon Common as Terry Eames starts to put a team together. (Paul Willatts)

After losing their winning run thanks to a 1-0 home defeat to Feltham, there was an eagerly anticipated showdown with Wallingford, but again the Dons fell flat when it mattered.

Sheerin was sent off in the first half for foul and abusive language, and they lost 3-0. It confirmed that they were lacking something to compete at the top. It was also a third defeat in a row after they were knocked out of the Premier Challenge Cup, the league cup, in the second round 5-1 by Southall the Saturday before.

December was a fruitful month, with five wins out of five as Cooper scored another seven goals – including his first hat-trick in a 5-0 win at Walton Casuals – but four points from three league games and losing 3-0 at home to Barkingside in the fourth round of the London Senior Cup brought a miserable January.

Confidence was restored with big wins over Westfield (5-0) and Chessington & Hook United (3-0) before a vital match with Withdean. With leaders Wallingford having withdrawn their application for Isthmian League status, a top-two finish could have still resulted in promotion, so victory was essential. But yet again the Dons could not match their opposition when it counted. They lost a bad-tempered match 2-0 and had Sean Daly sent off for a bad tackle.

They had sixteen matches left after that, and went on another incredible run of fifteen wins and one draw that was somehow not enough for promotion. Despite beating Wallingford 3-2 thanks to Matt Everard's goal, they could not catch them and ended four points behind the long-time leaders. It was Withdean who took the title though, after their own superb end-of-season run saw them leapfrog both Wimbledon and Wallingford to finish thirteen points ahead of the Dons.

With Withdean's ground being given to Brighton & Hove Albion, their lack of a permanent home meant they could not go up, and gave Wimbledon a glimmer of hope that they would instead. However, the Ryman League decided they would rather save a team from relegation, which meant the Dons stayed in the Combined Counties League.

Cooper, who scored eighteen goals in those final sixteen matches, ended the season top scorer with thirty-eight league goals and forty-three in total, with Sidwell winning both the players' and supporters' player of the year awards.

Throughout, there had been issues with where the Dons would play next season. Financially stricken Brentford had struck a deal with the Khosla family to groundshare Kingsmeadow with Kingstonian if they left their Griffin Park home – meaning the Dons would be homeless once more. Having seen a deal to expand and share Tooting & Mitcham's ground blocked, the Dons were grateful when Brentford chose to stay put. To stop the unnerving situation happening again and secure their long-term future, Wimbledon decided their best course of action was to buy Kingsmeadow. A deal worth £3 million was struck with the Khosla's on 25 June, and saw Wimbledon take over the 110-year lease with the freehold held by Kingston Council. It took until 2006 for the debt to Khosla to be paid off, when the club decided to borrow the money from Barclays Bank instead. It gave them a set payment plan, instead of paying money to Khosla on an ad hoc basic when they had raised it.

Although the agreement secured a future for Wimbledon, it did mean there would be no swift return to Merton, while Kingstonian stayed on as tenants. It was a turbulent but pleasing outcome and set the Dons up nicely for another assault on promotion.

Right: Terry Eames celebrates with fans and hails the crowd after AFC Wimbledon win their first competitive game at Sandhurst. (Paul Willatts)

Below: Record AFC Wimbledon goalscorer Kevin Cooper conquers the mud to score the second goal of his hat-trick at Chessington & Hook United in February. (Paul Willatts)

3

EAMES EXITS AS THE RISE BEGINS

Having had a season to acclimatise to their new surroundings in the Combined Counties League, AFC Wimbledon romped through it at the second attempt. They finished the campaign unbeaten, won promotion with seven games to go, celebrated a league and cup double and even enjoyed a long run in the FA Vase. And it all happened despite the upheaval of Terry Eames's sacking midway through.

All the big name players returned for the year, but pre-season started with a defeat to their now tenants Kingstonian (2-0). There were wins against Dorchester Town and Carshalton Athletic, but defeats to Division One side Watford (4-1) and Division Two side Luton Town (2-0), both at Kingsmeadow. They also lost 1-0 to Sutton United, who they faced in a repeat of their first-ever game twelve months earlier.

The league season kicked off on 16 August at Feltham and, having ended the previous campaign with a run of sixteen matches without defeat, Dons fans were understandably confident. There were four new faces in the starting XI, as goalkeeper Tony Smith, right-back Steve Gibson, midfielder Seb Favata and striker Wade Falana all made their debuts, as did Ryan Gray off the bench. They secured a comfortable 2-0 win with goals from Lee Sidwell and Matt Everard. It was the first of twenty-one straight league wins as Wimbledon dominated.

There were some hefty wins in that run, including three in a row in late September and early October. They beat Chessington & Hook United 6-0, Kevin Cooper scoring a hat-trick, Bedfont 6-1 and Chessington United 7-0, with Joe Sheerin netting three. Cooper scored three other hat-tricks, against Farnham Town, Raynes Park Vale and Walton Casuals, while Sheerin also scored three in the matches against Hartley Wintney and Merstham – a match where the Dons had been 2-0 down after eighteen minutes and came back to win 3-2. It was not the only scare they had, as they also had to score three late goals to beat Ash United 5-3. There was a debut for Michael Harvey, otherwise known as rap star MC Harvey from So Solid Crew, in a 3-0 win over Chipstead, where Simon Bassey was sent off.

Outside of the league, things were also going well in the cup competitions. Victories over Westfield (7-2), thanks to another Cooper hat-trick, and Pagham (1-0), despite another Bassey red card, put the Dons into the first round proper of the FA Vase. Everard ensured further progress with a last-minute winner in a 3-2 victory against Herne Bay, before more success against Wootton Blue Cross (3-0) and BAT Sports (1-0) secured a place in the fourth round. The Dons had also won twice in the Combined Counties

Premier Challenge Cup and once in the Surrey Senior Cup, but did go out of the London Senior Cup at the first hurdle, fielding a largely reserve side and losing 6-2 at Ilford.

By 10 January, the Dons had reached thirty games in all competitions and had won twenty-nine of them. But then they experienced something strange: back-to-back matches without victory. They returned to the scene of their first league game sixteen months earlier at Sandhurst Town, and came back with a 2-2 draw after Eames rested five first-team players, including Sidwell and Cooper, with the FA Vase fourth-round trip to North West Counties Division Two side Colne a week later. But even their return could not prevent a 2-1 loss as the Dons wasted a number of chances and saw their Vase hopes ended.

Despite also going out of the Surrey Senior Cup shortly after, when they lost 2-1 to Banstead Athletic, there was to be no wobble in the league or the Premier Challenge Cup, as the Dons beat Farnham Town, Feltham and Ash United in the league and Chipstead 3-1 in extra time in the cup.

Behind the scenes things were far from rosy though, as the relationship between the Dons Trust board and Eames deteriorated to the extent that he was suspended, and then sacked, for gross misconduct in February.

The approaches of the board and Eames had drifted in different directions, as Eames began to make his own decisions and ignore those of the board. When it suspended him on 13 February, a statement from the board said it could no longer trust Eames to be accountable and truthful to it, and set up a formal disciplinary hearing that centred around three charges. It said that between 6 and 9 February, he had lied to coaching staff, falsely told them the board would not support his plan for youth football and wanted him to make budget cuts, and that he had dispensed with members of the coaching staff citing false reasons.

The hearing was independent, as Eames could not appeal to the very board that had suspended him. He could not convince them of his honesty though and they ruled that he had deliberately lied to the board, lied to employees, cancelled youth football proposals to cause insult, took action instead of raising concerns, refused to give assurances he would not take unauthorised actions again and that his actions had damaged the reputation of the club. On 18 February, he was sacked, bringing a sad end to his and Wimbledon's relationship. Chief executive Kris Stewart took the brave decision to announce the sacking to the Wimbledon fans after a 5-0 Premier Challenge Cup quarter-final win over Raynes Park Vale, and took stick from those that did not understand it at the time.

Eames' assistant manager Nicky English was named caretaker manager and won his next five league games as the Dons scored twenty-four goals and conceded none. Chessington & Hook were swept aside 9-0, with Cooper scoring another hat-trick, and Bedfont 8-0, where Paul Scott scored his first AFC Wimbledon hat-trick. A 3-0 win over Westfield saw the Dons' goal difference reach +100.

The juggernaut slowed slightly with draws against Chipstead and nearest challengers AFC Wallingford in March. But, after that slight dip, they cantered to the title, winning thirteen of their final fourteen games, drawing only their penultimate match, against Reading Town, 3-3 thanks to a sixteenth-minute Cooper hat-trick.

The run included 6-0 wins against Withdean 2000, a shadow of the title-winning side from twelve months before, and Merstham, and an 8-0 win over Cove, in which

Cooper scored four times. There was a scare at Chessington & Hook, where the Dons were 3-1 down with fifteen minutes left before coming back to win 5-3. Both teams ended the game with nine men; Gareth Graham and Shane Small-King sent off for the Dons, while English was sent to the stands.

The league title was wrapped up on Easter Monday with a 3-0 win at Walton Casuals. With Wallingford only drawing with Reading Town in a morning kick-off, English's men knew victory would seal the championship. They showed no nerves and Everard and Cooper scored in the first twenty minutes, before Cooper added a third goal to spark wild celebrations at AFC Wimbledon's first title.

A second trophy followed, as the Dons made it a league and cup double. After the first game was abandoned due to crowd trouble with the score at 2-2, Wimbledon beat Coney Hall 5-0 in the Premier Challenge Cup semi-final, thanks to another Cooper hat-trick. It set up a final against North Greenford United and, although Wimbledon went behind, they came back to win 4-1. Gavin Bolger got the equaliser, Everard put them ahead and Cooper scored another two more to add to his remarkable tally for the season, ending on sixty-seven.

Scoring so many goals was not enough for Cooper, and he rounded off the season by proposing to his girlfriend, Sophie, in the centre circle after the final game against AFC Wallingford, switched to Kingsmeadow as the Oxfordshire side thought they would struggle with the crowd. She said yes. It was to be Cooper's final act in AFC Wimbledon colours.

Matt Everard, who turned down an approach from Conference side Aldershot in February to stay at Wimbledon, scored an impressive twenty-four goals from defence to finish as third-highest scorer that season, behind Sheerin on twenty-five. In total, the club racked up 130 points, winning forty-two and drawing four games, scoring 180 goals. Adding to their sixteen-game unbeaten run last season, they had now gone sixty-two league games without defeat.

Gavin Bolger enjoys the championship celebrations with the Wimbledon fans. (Paul Willatts)

AFC Wimbledon lift the Premier Challenge Cup after beating North Greenford United 4-1 in the final to complete a league and cup double. (Paul Willatts)

4

RECORD BREAKERS

AFC Wimbledon had the thirst for success, and even the step up to Isthmian League Division One South didn't stop them. Despite a new manager and new players, they stormed through the league – winning it in early April, earning a place in the record books and a second successive league and cup double on the way.

Nicky English had not lost a game as caretaker manager the previous season, but the board decided to bring in a fresh face. Dave Anderson joined only three days into the summer from Isthmian Premier League Hendon, and had the experience Wimbledon felt they needed to continue their ascent up the non-League pyramid. English accepted a job managing a new under-18 side alongside Keith Ward, but left the following summer. Former Wimbledon goalkeeper Dickie Guy was named club president, and physiotherapist Mike Rayner joined, staying with the club until 2013.

Danny Oakins, Andy Sullivan, Matt Martin, Seb Favata and Lee Sidwell all left the Dons, but it was another player's exit that grabbed all the headlines. Star striker Kevin Cooper wanted a contract, but Anderson had a policy of not offering one to anyone over twenty-five and Cooper was twenty-nine. Despite efforts to find an agreement, Cooper joined Conference South side Carshalton Athletic, two leagues higher up the pyramid. He had earned his spot in AFC Wimbledon's history though by scoring a remarkable 107 goals in 105 appearances, and was still their record goalscorer at the end of the 2012/13 season.

Simon Bassey made his last Dons appearance after a serious knee injury required an operation in the summer and was aggravated again when he played in a pre-season friendly. By October, it was clear he would not regain full fitness and Anderson named him player-coach. There was an influx of new players for pre-season, with Anderson using twenty-three players in his first friendly, a 1-0 away defeat against Dagenham & Redbridge, for whom a striker that Wimbledon fans would get to know very well, Jack Midson, started. Other friendlies included an impressive 3-0 win against Conference side Barnet, in which Robert Ursell celebrated signing a two-year contract (having turned down the offer of a trial with MK Dons) with a hat-trick, and a 2-0 defeat to Brentford that saw the League One side win the Supporters Direct Cup.

When the season started, Wimbledon were eyeing a special record. Two seasons earlier, Cornish side St Blazey had gone seventy-five games without defeat to win the South Western League, setting the record for English senior football in the process. Wimbledon had gone sixty-two matches since their last loss and knew another fourteen undefeated

Steve Butler heads home as AFC Wimbledon open their Isthmian Division One South campaign with a 5-1 win over Ashford Town (Kent). (Paul Willatts)

games would give them their place in history. Seven straight wins at the beginning of the season was a cracking way to start.

Two debutants made their mark in the opening match with Ashford Town (Kent) as strikers Jamie Taylor and Richard Butler both scored twice in a 5-1 romp at Kingsmeadow. There was a last-minute comeback at Horsham, where the Dons were losing 2-1 with a minute left, but won 3-2 thanks to a penalty from Ursell and a late Steve Butler header.

Joe Sheerin got his first goal of the season in a 3-1 win over Walton & Hersham – who were to be the Dons' nearest challengers in the league – but spent most the season injured.

Richard Butler's fine early season form made up for Cooper's departure and Sheerin's absence though, with the nineteen-year-old's double in the 3-0 win over Croydon taking his tally to seven goals in eight games.

The club were on form on all fronts, and transferred their league confidence to the FA Cup, a competition they had always had strong affiliations with following Wimbledon's 1988 win – an accomplishment celebrated in a replaying of the game in aid of the Dons Trust on 12 September between many of the Wimbledon and Liverpool players that had played at Wembley.

A preliminary qualifying-round match with Ashford Town (Kent) was AFC Wimbledon's debut in the competition, as new teams have to be registered for three seasons before they can enter. It was a successful debut as they comfortably won 3-0 with two Ursell goals. Richard Butler scored the other in that game and got another in the first qualifying round, as the Dons shocked Isthmian Premier League side Dover Athletic with a 1-0 win. There was another upset in the next round, and this time it was Southern League Premier side Dunstable Town that felt their wrath. Ursell scored all three goals in a 3-0 win, a hat-trick that earned him the player of the round award and a VIP seat to watch the final in Cardiff.

Some were starting to dream of an appearance in the first round proper, but those hopes were quashed by Conference South Thurrock, as they eased to a 2-0 victory at

Debutant Richard Butler celebrates the first of his two goals against Ashford Town (Kent). (Paul Willatts)

Kingsmeadow in the third qualifying round. It had though been an enjoyable return to the historic competition.

As well as debuting in the FA Cup, the Dons appeared in the FA Trophy for the first time – a competition open to clubs from the Conference down to Isthmian League level. Their form was not quite as good here though as, despite beating Met Police 2-0 in the qualifying round, they went out 3-0 to Anderson's former side Hendon in the first round. They did though progress in the league cup, known as the Bryco Cup, with a 2-0 win over Flackwell Heath and a 2-1 defeat of Horsham that saw Anderson sent from the dugout. They also beat Brimsdown Rovers 3-1 in the first round of the London Senior Cup.

Back in the league, Wimbledon's quest to break the record was still going strong. By the end of October, they had won nine and drawn three – including a 2-2 draw with Tooting & Mitcham – and taken their unbeaten run to seventy-four games.

Rob Ursell keeps his cool to score from the penalty spot in AFC Wimbledon's first FA Cup game. (Paul Willatts)

Players and management celebrate breaking the record for the longest unbeaten run in English senior football at Bromley. (Paul Willatts)

If they avoided defeat against Fleet Town on 2 November they knew they would equal St Blazey's record, and they did just that by winning 3-0 at Kingsmeadow with goals from Steve Butler, Richard Butler and Ryan Gray.

Due to their cup commitments, they had to wait eleven days for their chance to hold the record outright. It wasn't easy, as opponents Bromley pushed them all the way, taking the lead and enjoying sustained pressure at the end of the match. But Ursell's thirty-second-minute equaliser was enough for a 1-1 draw that wrote AFC Wimbledon's name into the record books, and sparked wild celebrations in the dressing room. It was another remarkable achievement for a club that had not existed two and a half years earlier.

The fans sang 'We are Invincible' during wins over Dulwich Hamlet (2-0) and Bashley (2-1), but all good things come to an end. At Cray Wanderers on 4 December, Anderson was hit heavily by injuries, with Ursell, Steve Gibson and Matt Everard (who was facing up to missing the rest of the season with an anterior cruciate ligament injury) out, and Chris Gell suspended. Top scorer Richard Butler was one of a number of players on the bench who were not match fit. It was a recipe for disaster and so it proved, with James Miller putting Cray ahead inside two minutes. The patched-up Dons dominated possession, but could not find an equaliser and Sam Wood sealed a 2-0 defeat with nineteen minutes left.

And so, after seventy-eight league games, the Dons' remarkable run, started on 26 February 2003, with a 3-1 win over Chessington United, was over. It is a record that still stood in 2013 and will take some beating.

All was not lost though, as the Dons were still the league's runaway leaders and in three cup competitions – the Bryco Cup, the London Senior Cup and the Surrey Senior Cup, which was yet to start.

Thumping wins over Molesey (4-0) and Ashford Town (Kent) (4-1), with Gary Prigent scoring twice in both games, had them back on track before a New Year's Day wobble at home to Whyteleafe. Former Dons Sullivan, Oakins, Sidwell and Paul Scott all played for Leafe, who won 2-1. Wimbledon was just playing with the rest of the league though, and won six and drew two of their next eight games to cement their position at the top. In the 3-0 win over Croydon, Ryan Gray was shown the Dons' only red card of the season for a late scuffle with Maroitt Lusengo, and had to wear a ball and chain during the end-of-season presentations as penance.

In the cup competitions, an under-strength Dons side had been dumped out of the London Senior Cup 4-0 at home by Fisher Athletic in January, and went out of the Bryco Cup at the quarter-final stage in February. A 4-2 defeat to Ryman Premier League side Slough Town was enough to end their run after the Dons had beaten Cray 3-2 in the previous round. They were through into the semi-finals of the Surrey Senior Cup, thanks to beating Chessington United 4-1, tenants Kingstonian 2-1 in the first competitive fixture between the two, and a young Crystal Palace side (which included future Eagles first-team players Rhoys Wiggins and Lewis Grabban) 2-0 with goals from young striker Andy Frost and Richard Butler.

Promotion had never really been in doubt, but Anderson made sure of it by making four new signings with ten games to go. It led to five straight wins, which guaranteed a top-two finish and promotion. One of those signings was New Zealander Shane Smeltz, who would become the Dons' first international. He scored twice on his debut, and missed a penalty, in a 5-0 win against Newport IOW and then scored again in a much-anticipated top-of-the-table clash at home to Horsham. Richard Butler scored twice to add to goals from Smeltz and Ursell in a 4-1 win that showed just how dominant the Dons were. That was followed by a 3-1 success over Banstead Athletic that meant Wimbledon needed one win from their remaining six matches for promotion.

Dorking were the visitors to an expectant Kingsmeadow on 28 March, and they were quickly put to the sword. Steve Butler's goal on seven minutes got the party started and, after it was added to by Sonny Farr's free-kick and Leon McDowell's late third for a 3-0 win, back-to-back promotions were guaranteed before Easter.

A 4-0 defeat to Walton & Hersham, going for the second promotion spot, briefly halted talk of the title, but the Dons got the point they needed by beating Met Police 1-0. Wins against Cray (3-0) and Burgess Hill Town (3-1), and a 1-1 draw with Tooting, which made the Terrors the only team Wimbledon had not beaten that season, rounded off the campaign. Wimbledon ended the season with ninety-seven points, nine clear of Walton & Hersham, and having lost just three times.

They weren't happy to stop there, and went hunting a double in the Surrey Senior Cup. Sutton United were their semi-final opponents and favourites, but that didn't stop Wimbledon as they won 1-0. Defender Anthony Howard was the unlikely hero, scoring

Steve Butler and Chris Gell celebrate a second successive league and cup double after beating Walton & Hersham in the Surrey Senior Cup final. (Paul Willatts)

the only goal of the game and then donning the 'keeper's gloves after Paul Smith was taken to hospital in the last minute with a dislocated shoulder. Anderson was also sent to the stands for kicking a water bottle after coach Warren Kelly had been dismissed.

The final was against Walton & Hersham at Kingsmeadow as the Dons eyed revenge for their recent defeat to the Swans. It was a close-run thing, but they got it. Smeltz put Wimbledon ahead, but a Neil Lampton penalty meant extra time, where Richard Butler was once more the hero when he converted Ursell's pass for a 2-1 win.

Butler ended the season as top scorer with thirty-one goals and won all four of the main player awards: Junior Dons' player of the year, young player of the year, WISA player of the year and players' player of the year. Howard made an impressive sixty-nine appearances including friendlies, while Anderson was named the Isthmian League Division One manager of the season to round off a satisfying campaign.

5
APPLYING THE BRAKES

After four trophies in two seasons, AFC Wimbledon were riding a wave of success, which came to a shuddering halt in the Isthmian Premier League. A league campaign plagued by inconsistency ended with defeat in the play-offs and in the Surrey Senior Cup final, as the Dons fell at the final hurdle on two fronts. There was an enjoyable run to the FA Trophy first round as well, but there was to be no addition to the trophy cabinet this time.

Before the season started, Dave Anderson signed a three-year contract and set about reshuffling his squad, signing twelve new players. Only Simon Sobihy, goalkeeper Andy Little, Wayne Finnie, Dave Sargent and Wes Daly would make a consistent impact though. Out of the door went Gavin Bolger, Martin Randall, Steve Gibson, Chris Gell, Danny Naisbitt, Gareth Graham and Joe Sheerin – who joined Croydon Athletic to bring an end to a three-year relationship that went back to the first trials on Wimbledon Common. Leon McDowell went on loan to Croydon Athletic, but in January was sentenced to two years in jail for robbing West Ham United defender Anton Ferdinand of two mobile phones. Robert Ursell tore his posterior cruciate ligament in a close-season run and was ruled out for four months, while Matt Everard was forced to retire when told he needed a second operation on his anterior cruciate ligament injury. When the season started, Ryan Gray was the only surviving member from the Dons' Combined Counties League days, but he left soon after, having struggled to juggle work and football. Craig Carley, who played for the Dons in their first season, did return, but only played twice before leaving again. There was also a brief return for left-back Michael Harvey.

One person going nowhere was Simon Bassey. Coaching the reserves alongside Johnny Morris and Dave Wager, he was winning plenty of admirers, but turned down offers to manage elsewhere to stay with Wimbledon.

It didn't take long for Anderson's new boys to bed in and get to know each other. After a successful pre-season, which included winning the Supporters Direct Cup 1-0 against FC United and drawing 1-1 with Conference side Aldershot Town – managed by future Dons hero Terry Brown – they started the new season in typical dominant fashion, winning their first three games before drawing the next three 1-1. Little, Daly, Sargent, Finnie, Matt York and Amadou Kouman were full debutants in the opening match against Folkestone Invicta, while Matt Fowler and Barry Moore came off the bench in a 4-1 win in which Shane Smeltz scored twice.

Over the next two months, Wimbledon's league fortunes were mixed. Six of their first eleven games ended 1-1, and they lost 2-1 at home to Worthing and 2-1 at table-toppers Hampton & Richmond, a match Wimbledon dominated but had Steve Butler sent off in.

Even Wimbledon's cup runs were inconsistent. In the FA Cup, they needed a replay to get past Ashford Town (Middlesex) in the first qualifying round, winning the second game 2-0 with Richard Butler scoring once to celebrate a new contract. But their 3-0 loss to Walton & Hersham in the next round left Anderson furious. He told his players to take a long look around the changing room, as they might not be in it again.

There was no success in the Westview League Cup or London Senior Cup either. Having beaten Staines Town 2-0 in the first round of the League Cup, they crashed out 1-0 at home to Hendon, having already lost 3-2 against Wingate & Finchley in the London Cup.

They fared better in the FA Trophy though, by making the first round proper for the season successive season. A 1-0 win over King's Lynn thanks to Anthony Howard's winner, and a 2-1 victory over Ramsgate set up a third qualifying-round tie with Southern League Eastern Division side Dartford. Again, the Dons needed a replay, after a goalless first game in Kent, where Richard Butler and Moore scored in the final five minutes for a 2-0 win and a place in the first round. They were drawn against Conference South high-flyers St Albans City, which was also going to be a tough test, but the Dons came close to an upset. Richard Butler put them ahead and, although St Alban's hit back to lead 2-1, Sargent's penalty had the scores level. But when Moore bundled a low cross into his own net, there was no coming back and, to make matters worse, Harvey and Daly were both sent off after the final whistle.

With the cup games coming thick and fast between October and December, Wimbledon's league form was sporadic as they won six, drew four and lost three. There was a disappointing 2-0 loss away at Bromley, where Fowler was sent off for

AFC Wimbledon parade their new signings. Left to right: Sonny Farr, Josh Lennie, Andy Little, manager Dave Anderson, Matt York and Barry Moore. (Newsquest)

Shane Smeltz was AFC Wimbledon's first international player. He scored twice in the 4-1 win over Folkestone Invicta in the first game of the 2005/06 season. (Newsquest)

Richard Butler and Michael Harvey, of rap group So Solid Crew, celebrate Butler's goal, which put AFC Wimbledon ahead in the FA Trophy against St Albans City. (Newsquest)

headbutting the 'keeper; a 1-0 defeat at Chelmsford City in which Steve Butler and Howard both saw red; and a goalless draw at Leyton where the recently returned Chris Gell got his marching orders. Having only had one sending-off the previous campaign, the Dons already had six before Christmas. There were good results too, particularly a 4-0 win at Windsor & Eton where Richard Butler scored twice, and a 5-0 thumping of bottom-of-the-table Redbridge in a match stopped for ten minutes because mist shrouded both goals.

All that meant that, by the turn of the year, Wimbledon just had the league and the Surrey Senior Cup – which they started their defence of with a 3-2 win at home to Ash United – to concentrate on. Consistency continued to be the problem though. One week they would beat a high-flier and the next lose to a struggler. They beat promotion rivals Staines Town 3-0 with goals from Ursell, Sargent and Richard Butler, and also drew 1-1 with leaders Braintree Town, when captain Steve Butler scored a late equaliser after Paul Lorraine had put Braintree ahead in the last minute of normal time. But there was a 1-0 defeat to struggling Folkestone, a 2-1 defeat to Margate, and a 1-1 draw against second-bottom Windsor & Eton. It was a period that left Anderson – facing six weeks without top scorer Richard Butler, who needed a hernia operation, and even longer without cruciate ligament victim Simon Sweeney – admitting the play-offs looked a long way off.

But Wimbledon have never been a club who know when they are beaten, and bit by bit they clawed their way back into contention as they found the consistency they craved. A 1-0 win over second-placed Fisher Athletic thanks to Daly's goal was followed by a goalless draw with leaders Braintree that boosted confidence, and began a run of five wins from six and success in the Surrey Senior Cup.

Although Chelmsford City became only the second team to ever complete the league double over the Dons, winners from Dwayne Plummer (signed from Staines earlier in the season) in 1-0 victories against Margate and promotion rivals Heybridge Swifts, and goals from Smeltz and Daly in a 2-1 win over Harrow Borough, saw Wimbledon jump back into the play-offs for the first time in four months. Against Harrow there was a debut off the bench for Paul Barnes, an in-demand striker signed from Barton Rovers. He was brought in to replace the injured Richard Butler, and set about doing just that by scoring a hat-trick in only his third appearance, a 5-1 win over Wealdstone that took the Dons fourth. They were also into the last four of the Surrey Senior Cup, having beaten a Met Police side that included former favourite Kevin Cooper 2-0, and Combined Counties side Guildford City 4-0 in the quarter-finals with goals from Smeltz, Ursell, Mark King and Daly.

As the season entered the final stretch, everything was looking up, but then the Dons almost self-combusted, with back-to-back defeats against Hampton & Richmond and Billericay Town. 'Keeper Little was sent off for two bookings in three minutes in the 4-0 home defeat to Hampton, while Smeltz and Plummer were both red carded for striking out in the 2-1 loss at Billericay, which meant they would miss the final two games of the season and the play-off semi-final if Wimbledon got there. With other results going their way, Wimbledon were still in with a shout if they could finish the final four games well.

If there was any pressure, it didn't show, as they won all four. A dramatic ninety-fourth-minute Howard goal earned a 3-2 win over East Thurrock United after the Dons had been 2-0 up, and goals from Barnes and the fit-again Richard Butler resulted in a 2-0 win over

Walton & Hersham. When Butler scored the only goal of the game against Hendon, a play-off spot was secure with a game remaining. Tony Battersby and Barnes strikes saw them end the regular season with a 2-1 win over Harrow Borough, and secure fourth place and a play-off semi-final at third-placed Fisher Athletic, whom they had finished eight points behind.

Success in the Surrey Senior Cup meant Dons fans were in for a thrilling end-of-season finale, as a 2-1 win over Ashford Town (Middlesex) in the semi-final, with goals from Ursell and Smeltz, set up a final against their Kingsmeadow tenants Kingstonian.

Momentum is the buzzword in the play-offs and the Dons had it, with four straight wins and the knowledge that they had twice beaten Fisher 1-0 in the regular season. But Fisher had been Anderson's tip to win the league and the Dons had a crippling injury list that, in the end, proved too much to overcome. Despite Howard's seventy-eighth-minute goal, earlier strikes from Leroy Griffiths and Steve Watts put Fisher through 2-1. Fisher went on to get promotion by beating Hampton 3-0 in the final, but it was scant consolation.

Worse was to come in the Surrey Senior Cup, as Wimbledon and Isthmian Division One South Kingstonian faced off at Woking's ground ten days after the play-off disappointment. The Dons dominated for large periods, but Martyn Lee's deflected free-kick denied them back-to-back trophies. Such was the disappointment, Anderson and the returning Smeltz gave their runners-up medals away.

Andy Little was named Junior Dons' player of the year and WISA player of the year, while Wes Daly was players' player of the year and Richard Butler, who ended the season as top scorer for a second year in a row with twenty-three goals, one more than Smeltz, the young player of the year.

Having aimed for the play-offs, Wimbledon had achieved their goal in one sense, but to end the campaign without a trophy, when they had become used to silverware, was a major disappointment.

AFC Wimbledon's wall holds firm in the play-off semi-final against Fisher Athletic, but the Dons were beaten 2-1 nevertheless. (Paul Willatts)

Paul Barnes is denied in the Surrey Senior Cup final defeat to Kingsmeadow tenants Kingstonian. (Newsquest)

Wes Daly and teammates in a dejected mood after the cup defeat that meant they ended the season without any trophies. (Newsquest)

6
THE DARLINGTON AFFAIR

After missing out on promotion, the Dons were desperate for a shot at the title, but again fell short in a campaign dominated by another battle with the Football Association and the Isthmian League, five years after the first.

The drama surrounding the signing of former Wimbledon player Jermaine Darlington and the resultant points penalty took away from the fact that the Dons had a pretty good season on the pitch. They enjoyed excellent runs in both the FA Cup and the FA Trophy – beating Conference sides Aldershot Town and Gravesend & Northfleet – and made the Isthmian Premier League play-offs again, despite the off-field pantomime. Promotion was the aim though, and when it didn't come, Dave Anderson lost his job.

Anderson's departure was one of many off-pitch developments by the following summer. Founding members Kris Stewart and Trevor Williams resigned from their jobs as chief executive and club secretary, with Williams blaming himself for the mistake that led to the Darlington affair. Stewart needed a break after almost five years at the helm, but has continued to be involved with the Dons Trust board. Erik Samuelson stood down as finance director at the start of the season, and temporarily replaced Stewart before being given the job permanently following his impressive handling of the Darlington case.

There were other issues off the pitch too. Irish businessman Darragh MacAnthony wanted to buy the club, offering funds for the playing budget, to bring in a professional management team and to orchestrate a move back to a stadium in Merton. He didn't grasp the fan-base ethos of AFC Wimbledon though, and was rejected, going on to buy Peterborough United instead. The scenario did get Wimbledon thinking about the direction of their club and started a discussion about the best way for them to achieve their goals of Football League football back in Merton.

While all this went on off the pitch, things went very well on it. Anderson, who promoted Simon Bassey to first-team coach, did his best to keep his squad from the previous year together, but did lose Shane Smeltz, Rob Ursell, Dwayne Plummer and Dave Sargent. Smeltz was sold to Conference side Halifax Town, Plummer moved to Braintree and Sargent was released. Ursell said he had fallen out of love with football, and moved to Windsor & Eton in September to try and rediscover his spark.

Among the players coming in the revolving Kingsmeadow door were experienced midfielder Steve Watson, left-sided player Michael Haswell, midfielder Steve Wales, Grenadian international Byron Bubb and former Crystal Palace striker Roscoe Dsane, who was to fill Smeltz's boots.

Haydon the Womble became the club's new mascot at the start of the 2006/07 season. Wimbledon FC's mascot had been Wandle the Womble. (Newsquest)

An underwhelming pre-season saw the Supporters Direct Cup go to FC United, who won the annual match 2-1, and Aldershot, conquered later in the season in the FA Trophy, leaving Kingsmeadow with a 4-1 win. However, the Dons enjoyed an impressive opening half of the campaign, not losing for their first nine games and reaching the halfway point of the season having only lost three times.

The new strike pairing of Richard Butler and Dsane both scored in an opening-day 2-1 win over Carshalton Athletic, but would go on to have very different seasons, with Butler missing a lot of it through a pelvic injury and Dsane ending as top scorer. Promising young winger Robin Shroot made his debut a 2-1 win over Ashford Town (Middlesex) that also saw Simon Sweeney return to the squad for the first time since his knee ligament injury. Hampton & Richmond continued to be the Dons' bogey team, when Lawrence Yaku's goal gave them a 1-0 win at Kingsmeadow, meaning the Beavers had now played Wimbledon three times in two seasons and won all three games.

With Wales fracturing his ankle and joining Butler on the treatment table, injuries were a big problem for the Dons, but they proved they had strength in depth, with a disappointing 3-0 defeat at Billericay Town their only blip. On-loan Brentford striker Scott Fitzgerald scored a hat-trick in the 3-1 win over Walton & Hersham that rounded off 2006, while reserve-team striker Stephen Goddard was making his mark in the first team by scoring a double in a 3-0 win over Chelmsford City – who had beaten the Dons 2-1 just two weeks earlier. It was all looking good for the Dons as they challenged at the top in the league, but it was in the cup competitions they really excelled.

In the FA Cup, the Dons came close to a first-ever appearance in the first round proper. Their campaign started with a 1-0 win over Horsham and 3-0 win over Oxhey Jets in the opening two qualifying rounds – striker Darren Grieves, signed from East Thurrock United in the summer, scoring in both. A 2-1 win over Evesham United in the third round, where Watson made his debut after injury, and goals from Paul Barnes and Bubb, who won the player of the round award and VIP tickets for the final just like Ursell two seasons before, set up a fourth qualifying-round tie away at Conference big boys Exeter City on 28 October. It was billed as AFC Wimbledon's biggest cup game since their formation, and saw them back on the national stage with coverage throughout the media. More than 1,500 Dons fans made the trip and almost saw their side grab a replay. After Andy Taylor scored a tap-in at the back post to put Exeter ahead after seven minutes, and Jon Challinor scored a beautiful curled second goal, the Dons were up against it. But they attacked from the off in the second half and Dsane pulled a goal back after beating the offside trap. The striker and Watson both went close, as the Dons pushed for an equaliser that wouldn't come, and they exited the competition. They could hold their heads high though, having pushed the Grecians all the way.

The Dons were beaten 1-0 by Tooting & Mitcham in the third round of the Westview League Cup, and 3-2 at home to Dulwich Hamlet in the first round of the London Senior Cup, as a young side let a 2-0 lead slip. They were once more doing well in the Surrey Senior Cup though, thanks to a Goddard hat-trick in a 4-2 win over Banstead Athletic and Shroot's winner in a 2-1 victory over Met Police.

It was in the FA Trophy that the Dons really made their mark. Victories over Dunstable Town (2-1), with goals from Dsane and Barnes, and Tonbridge Angels (3-2), thanks to Luke Garrard and Barnes strikes added to by a John Beales own goal, put the Dons into the final qualifying round. Darlington was not included in the team against Angels but had

Lawrence Yaku (far left) celebrates scoring against the Dons, as Hampton & Richmond continued to be their bogey team. It was the Beavers' third win out of three games between the two teams. (Newsquest)

made the squad for the first time. The thirty-two-year-old, who made 104 appearances for Wimbledon between 2001 and 2004, had been training with the Dons since the summer to regain fitness after injury and his release from Welsh Championship side Cardiff City. He made his debut in a 1-0 league win over Harrow Borough at home on 11 November, playing seventy-seven minutes and then agreeing terms to stay at the club until the end of the season. He became the first player to play for both Wimbledon and AFC Wimbledon.

The final qualifying round saw Wimbledon drawn against Conference South side Eastleigh at Kingsmeadow. After Eastleigh had gone ahead, Dsane forced a replay by equalising from Sweeney's cross for a 1-1 draw, despite Shroot's red card for two bookings. It set up what was to be a dramatic replay at Eastleigh. Once more, the Dons came from behind, as Fitzgerald tapped home Lewis Cook's cross in injury time for another 1-1 scoreline that forced extra time. The same combination again put the Dons ahead, only for Eastleigh to be the ones that this time equalised and brought about penalties. Up stepped goalkeeper Andy Little to produce some heroics and save twice from David Hughes and Darren Wheeler, before Wes Daly powered home the winning kick for a place in the first round proper against Aldershot.

If the FA Cup game against Exeter had been the biggest cup game in Wimbledon's history, then the shock victory over Aldershot on 16 December ran it close. Fitzgerald was again the hero, scoring the winner after Dsane's shot was parried by Aldershot's Nikki Bull for a 2-1 win, with Chris Gell having earlier put Wimbledon back on level terms. It was another special day in Wimbledon's history, but was eclipsed almost immediately in the second round. The Dons went to high-flying Conference South Gravesend & Northfleet on 13 January and once more produced a huge shock, winning 1-0 with Dsane on the scoresheet.

The Dons were in ecstasy, challenging for the promotion in the Isthmian Premier League and into the last sixteen of the FA Trophy for the first time. But it was all about to come crashing down around them.

Five days after beating Gravesend, Wimbledon announced on their website that the FA had asked for clarification as to the status of one of their players. That player was Darlington. When a player switches from a Welsh club to an English club like Darlington did, they change FAs and need an international transfer certificate when they are registered, and Wimbledon had not got one. It was a simple oversight from club secretary Williams, and nobody spotted the error until Darlington was booked for the first time in his AFC Wimbledon career against Gravesend. When the FA went to record the booking, they found no record of the player. It started two months of chaos, in which it appeared everyone wanted to hang Wimbledon out to dry.

On 19 January, Wimbledon were charged with fielding an ineligible player against Gravesend and six days later found guilty. The FA took the opportunity to throw the rule book at them, by chucking them out of the Trophy and demanding they repay the prize money won against Eastleigh, Aldershot and Gravesend, the games Darlington had played in. Wimbledon were furious; a simple administrative error was being punished as a deliberate effort to pull the wool over the authorities eyes.

In the meantime, the Isthmian League decided to jump on the bandwagon too. On 7 February, they found the Dons guilty of fielding a player before having obtained an international transfer certificate, which therefore also meant they were guilty of fielding an ineligible player in the league. If the FA's punishment seemed harsh, then the league's was outrageous, as they docked the Dons all eighteen points they had won when Darlington had played and fined them £400. It was a penalty that dropped the Dons from fourth to thirteenth, ending any chance of promotion, and had everyone connected to the club fuming. Not long after, the Surrey FA threw the Dons out of the Surrey Senior Cup as well, for fielding Darlington against Banstead and Met Police. There was no appeal process here and Anderson said the club should never enter the competition again.

It all left a sour taste around Wimbledon and they released a statement saying they would be appealing the Isthmian League and the FA's decisions.

> We are very disappointed, but not surprised, that the FA has not answered our questions but has, instead, said 'rules is rules'.
>
> We first intend to exhaust our remedies within football, but we believe that grounds exist to bring proceedings against the FA in the High Court, or even the European Court, and we shall consider those options once the process within football is completed. The same route remains open to us regarding the Isthmian League decision if our appeal fails.

When they lodged their appeal, Wimbledon pointed to the fact that Darlington was registered and they had only committed a technical breach of the rules; that it was a victimless crime with no intended deception; and that they had been disproportionately punished compared to clubs such as Liverpool and West Ham, who had committed a similar offence and been punished less.

Jermaine Darlington makes his home debut against Tonbridge Angels. His signing was a controversial one that brought about another battle with the Football Association. (Newsquest)

The decision to reduce Wimbledon's points deduction from eighteen points to three sparked jubilant scenes at Kingsmeadow when they beat Slough Town 9-0. (Newsquest)

It took more than a month for the FA to hear Wimbledon's appeal and their case, as well as the Isthmian League's. But on 26 March, it was announced the penalty was being reduced from eighteen points to three, leaving the Isthmian League, and the likes of chairman Alan Turvey, who sat on the independent commission back in 2002, livid enough to produce their own hard-hitting statement.

> The decision of the FA confirms that the League acted correctly and that it did not misinterpret its own League Rule and that the deduction of 18 points was wholly in accordance with the Rules. The FA also confirmed that the League correctly interpreted the meaning of 'shall' in Rule 6.8, which provides that 'Any club found to have played an ineligible player in a match shall have any points gained from that match deducted from its record.
>
> It is therefore difficult to understand how the Appeal Board can make such a finding and then vary the decision of the League.

Wimbledon though were happy and, as far as they were concerned, had reached the end of the matter, declining to go further to the High Court and instead concentrate on getting their promotion hopes back on track. It had been a turbulent time, but once more AFC Wimbledon had battled the authorities and come out on top.

Despite the spectre of the points penalty, Wimbledon's progress in the league remained solid, and they put together a ten-game winning run from mid-January until early March.

Wales scored in a 1-1 draw with Horsham that took them top in February and then scored twice more when they beat promotion rivals Billericay Town 3-2. Paul Lorraine scored the other, having been brought in on loan from Fisher Athletic as cover over the Christmas season but impressing enough to stay until the end of the season.

It was remarkable the players had kept their heads on the pitch, given all that had happened off it and, inevitably, they imploded, taking one point from three games, losing a top-of-the-table clash at bogey side Hampton & Richmond 2-1. Debutant Lee O'Leary, signed from Hendon after impressing against the Dons when they beat them 3-1 two weeks earlier, was sent off for a bad tackle in the first half. Hampton leapfrogged Wimbledon into second, but two days later the Dons got the boost they needed when they found out they were being deducted three points and not eighteen. It pushed them down to fifth, the final play-off spot, two points ahead of Margate.

The lesser points deduction was celebrated enthusiastically both on and off the pitch. A day after the announcement, the Dons beat Leyton 5-2 with Steven Ferguson, signed from Woking, scoring twice and Dsane, O'Leary and a fit-again Richard Butler also finding the net. That was followed by a home match against Slough Town that saw fans celebrating not only the result of the appeal, but also a huge 9-0 win. Anthony Howard, later named WISA player of the year and players' player of the year, scored a hat-trick, and debutant Richard Jolly, a striker signed from Heybridge Swifts, got on the scoresheet as well. Jolly's arrival saw Barnes join Arlesey Town.

The Dons had hit form at the right time and ended the final five games of the season undefeated to clinch a play-off spot. There had still been hopes of the title, but draws against Boreham Wood (0-0) and Staines Town (1-1) ended those, while Dsane's twenty-first goal of the season, a penalty that secured a 1-1 draw at home to Heybridge, meant the Dons went into the final game of the season in the final play-off spot only a point ahead of Margate. They knew a win would see them in and they got just that, by beating East Thurrock 4-0, Jolly scoring twice, O'Leary once and Wes Daly once.

And so Wimbledon finished fifth, seven points behind champions Hampton and knowing they would have been third and facing Chelmsford at home in the semi-finals without the points deduction. Instead, they were away to Bromley, a team they had beaten 3-1 and 3-2 during the regular season. Again, they had the momentum, having not lost in seven games, but once more they failed to make the final as they crashed out 1-0. Daly was the villain of the piece, as he was sent off for two bookings in the thirty-fifth minute, leaving his teammates with a mountain to climb. Assistant manager Jon Turner was also sent to the stands during the game, won by Nic McDonnell's header in the second half. Jolly had the chance to force extra time, but lobbed over an empty goal with the last kick of the game to leave Wimbledon facing another year in the Isthmian League.

It marked the end of the road for Dave Anderson. Anderson had promised Conference South football after two years in the Premier League, but hadn't delivered and paid the price as he was sacked. He knew what was coming and left amicably. In three years in charge, he had won Division One South and the Surrey Senior Cup in his first year, but had remained trophy-less after that. He had twice reached the play-offs and was unlucky both times, being hit by injuries in 2006 against Fisher and by Daly's red card against Bromley, but it wasn't enough to prolong his Wimbledon stay.

Dave Anderson confronts the referee after a 2-0 defeat to Hampton & Richmond that saw Lee O'Leary sent off on his debut. (Newsquest)

Wes Daly hangs his head after his sending-off in the play-off semi-final defeat to Bromley, which ultimately cost Dave Anderson his job. (Paul Willatts)

7

BROWN'S BOYS

After two years in the Isthmian League, AFC Wimbledon were desperate to get out and carry on their progress back to the Football League. In 2008, they finally managed it. The season was not without its dramas though, with a new manager, a new record signing, a contract dispute, a goalkeeping crisis, the departure of two long-serving favourites, an appearance at Wembley and another run to the last sixteen of the FA Trophy – not to mention a thrilling play-off final.

The biggest problem at the start of the year was finding a manager to replace Dave Anderson. There was plenty of interest in the job, but it didn't take long for the Dons to pick their main. Terry Brown had left Aldershot in March after five years in charge, taking them from the Isthmian Premier League to two Conference play-off finals. That record appealed to the Dons board and it was a journey they hoped he could repeat with them. He brought with him his long-term assistant Stuart Cash, and kept Simon Bassey as first-team coach before quickly stamping his mark on the squad.

His first signing was a familiar one, as he tempted Wimbledon FC legend Marcus Gayle to Kingsmeadow. The thirty-seven-year-old had played 285 games for Wimbledon and twelve months earlier had signed for Brown at Aldershot. He was followed by experienced defender Jason Goodliffe, right-back Will Salmon and five midfielders in Sam Hatton, Robert Quinn, Kevin Warner, Tony Finn and Karl Beckford. Just before pre-season they were added to by Jake Leberl and target man Daniel Webb, son of Chelsea's David Webb.

Youngsters Robin Shroot, Steve Goddard and Chris Hussey all signed up, but Paul Lorraine, Roscoe Dsane and Wes Daly all wanted full-time football and left for Woking, League Two Accrington Stanley and Maidenhead United. Other players on their way out were Steve Butler, Lee O'Leary, Steve Wales, Chris Gell, Simon Sweeney and Lewis Cook. Jermaine Darlington was also released as Brown targeted younger legs.

Kingsmeadow was renamed the Cherry Red Records Fans' Stadium when corporate sponsors Cherry Red Records decided to also sponsor the ground, and reserve team manager John Morris left to join Walton Casuals.

Pre-season was mixed, but saw Gayle score in his first appearance back in Wimbledon colours when the Dons beat Tooting & Mitcham 4-1. They also won the Supporters Direct Cup back as Webb and Finn goals beat FC United 2-0.

When the Dons lined up against Ramsgate for the opening game of the season, Brown's revolution was clear for all to see, with nine new names in the sixteen-man squad – one

Sam Hatton was one of nine new players in the squad for Terry Brown's first game in charge against Ramsgate. He marked his debut with two goals in a 2-0 win. (Newsquest)

of them securing victory. Hatton's two first-half goals were enough for a 2-0 win that was followed by a 2-1 victory at Wealdstone, thanks to Jolly and Webb strikes. Brown had started at a blistering pace, but then struggled, with only two points from the next five matches, forcing his hand into another player rejig. He transfer-listed Jolly after the striker chose to attend a friend's wedding rather than travel for the 2-2 draw at Leyton, and Warner left as he was not able to commit enough time to the club. In their places came Barnet striker Guiliano Grazioli, on a five-week loan, and experienced midfielder Mark Beard, who had played in the Conference for Stevenage Borough the season before.

The Dons needed a pick-me-up and got it in the first qualifying round of the FA Cup when they thumped Cray Wanderers 6-2, with Beckford and Finn both scoring twice to spark a run of eight games unbeaten in the league.

Richard Butler scored his first goal of the season in a 2-0 win over Maidstone United, where the ever-more-impressive Shroot set up both goals, and Finn nabbed the first hat-trick of the season in the 3-1 win at Harlow Town. He scored again in the 1-0 win over AFC Hornchurch, in which defender Luke Garrard played the second half in goal after Andy Little

Richard Butler celebrates his goal against Maidstone United, but his AFC Wimbledon career was coming to an end after failing to fit into Terry Brown's plans. He would face them in the play-off final at the end of the season. (Newsquest)

broke two fingers and dislocated another two. It put Wimbledon into fifth, but started a goalkeeping crisis. Paul Seuke, brought in as cover for Little in the summer, had been allowed to join Horsham, so teenager Corrin Brooks-Meade was signed on loan from Fulham, only to get injured on debut against Tonbridge Angels. Danny Knowles replaced him on loan from Grays Athletics, but Tottenham loanee Lee Butcher and Eastleigh's James Pullen also had spells between the sticks before the end of the season.

The Tonbridge game was important for another reason. It saw striker Jon Main score twice in a 2-2 draw against the Dons, before agreeing to join them for a club record fee in the region of £20,000. Brown hailed him as the missing piece to his AFC Wimbledon puzzle and he would go on to follow fellow strikers Kevin Cooper and Richard Butler – who left not long after the start of the season as he didn't fit into Brown's playing style – in becoming a fans' favourite thanks to an impressive goal tally.

After thumping Debenham LC 5-1 in the second round of the FA Cup, the Dons went out on penalties at the next stage. A goalless first tie against fellow Ryman Premier side Horsham at Kingsmeadow was followed by a 1-1 draw that meant spot-kicks. With the scores level at 4-4, Mark Beard smashed his effort over the bar and Lee Carney held his nerve to put Horsham through.

It was not the only cup disappointment, with early exits in both the Westview League Cup and Surrey Senior Cup at the hands of Whyteleafe, who won the league cup game 2-0, and then the Surrey Cup match 4-3 on penalties after a 0-0 draw.

Once more, the FA Trophy provided the cup excitement. Mark de Bolla marked his debut after signing from Ebbsfleet with the winning goal from the penalty spot in a 2-1 win over Hendon in the first qualifying round, which was followed by a 4-0 thrashing of ten-man Chelmsford City with Webb, de Bolla, Leberl and Finn all scoring. Hatton and Leberl goals then put them into the first round proper with a 2-1 win over Northwood.

In the league, the Dons were playing for second place after runaway league leaders Chelmsford avenged their Trophy defeat and moved thirteen points clear by beating Wimbledon 1-0 at the start of December. Over a productive Christmas and New Year programme, they made sure everyone knew they wanted that runners-up spot by winning five straight games with Main scoring four goals in as many matches.

One absentee during the impressive run was Shroot, who had been sent on loan to Harrow Borough in early November. By January, he was slapped on the transfer list when he would not sign a new contract and instead wanted a move to Harrow. It sparked a stand-off between player and club, with Wimbledon not wanting to sell him to promotion rivals Harrow and Shroot refusing to go to any of the clubs that met the asking price.

Either side of the five-game winning run, the Dons progressed through two more rounds of the Trophy. Having beaten Conference South side Maidenhead United 2-0 in the first round, with Gayle scoring his first competitive goal for the club, Tonbridge Angels were swept aside 4-0 in the second, with de Bolla scoring twice and missing a penalty. It put them through to the last sixteen for the second year running and this time they would get to play the game.

Torquay United were the visitors to Kingsmeadow on 2 February, and proved too good, as the Conference side won 2-0. Former Don Dsane scored the Gulls' first from the penalty spot on the ground where he had finished the previous season as top scorer. Tim Sills missed another penalty before Lee Phillips added a late second in a game where Wimbledon pushed their more illustrious opponents, who would go on to lose the final 1-0 to Ebbsfleet, all the way. Wimbledon's cup hopes for the year were ended completely three days later when they exited the London Senior Cup with a 4-1 defeat at Bromley.

So by mid-February the Dons had just the league to concentrate on. They had lost ground in January when they lost 3-2 at lowly Folkestone Invicta and 1-0 at home to Boreham Wood, where Pullen made his debut and injury reduced the Dons to just twelve regular first-team players. One of those missing was Main, who broke a metatarsal in his foot after scoring twice in a 2-2 draw with his former employers Tonbridge.

Fears they were about to drop away proved dumbfounded though, as seven wins in eight games nearly confirmed a play-off spot and brought the gap to Chelmsford back down to eight points. Luis Cumbers, signed on loan from Gillingham, was proving an adequate replacement for Main, scoring in four straight games, including thumpings of bottom club Leyton 5-0 and Wealdstone 6-1. A 4-0 win over Hastings United saw a sad goodbye to the club's longest servant, however. When Richard Butler left, Antony Howard

Antony Howard shadows former teammate Roscoe Dsane when Torquay United visit Kingsmeadow in the third round of the FA Trophy. (Newsquest)

was the last survivor of the squad that had won Ryman Division One South three seasons earlier, but he too was now on his way, having been offered a coaching role in New York. He left with the club's blessing after four seasons.

With the gap at the top reduced, the Dons had the scent of automatic promotion again, when they travelled to Chelmsford in a match billed as the biggest game of the season. With ten minutes left, it looked like Wimbledon might reduce the gap to five points, as they had come from behind to lead 2-1 thanks to a Steve Clark own goal and Garrard penalty. But Chelmsford underlined their superiority by equalising with a penalty of their own, and then striking a winner with four minutes left to secure a 3-2 win. It meant that if Wimbledon wanted promotion, they would have to go through the dreaded play-offs.

Brown freshened up the squad by bringing in striker Elliott Buchanan from Stevenage and Nic McDonnell, the man who scored against the Dons in the play-offs the previous season, on dual registration with Bromley. Sammon, Jolly, de Bolla and Beckford all left on loan. One other player returning to Kingsmeadow was Shroot. A spell of eight goals in eleven games for Harrow earned him a recall to the Dons and it proved a master stroke, as his injury-time winner secured a 2-1 victory over Billericay Town that kept the Dons six points clear of third-placed Staines. He did even better in the next game against Ashford Town (Middlesex), with a hat-trick in a 4-1 win where Main made his comeback.

The day after that game, Wimbledon appeared at Wembley in a special match against Corinthian Casuals to mark their opponent's 125-year anniversary – it was also twenty years since Wimbledon's FA Cup triumph. Many youngsters and fringe players played, as did Simon Bassey, and the Dons won 8-1.

Back in the league, they blew their advantage in the race for second by losing 2-1 at Harlow Town in their penultimate game, and seeing Staines move above them. Main got back on the scoresheet in the final match against fourth-placed AFC Hornchurch that ended 1-1 in a dress rehearsal for the play-off semi-finals. The Dons finished third, three points behind Bromley and twelve behind Chelmsford.

Despite taking four points off Hornchurch during the season, Wimbledon fans were nervous after two successive play-off semi-final defeats. Only three players in the squad had played against Bromley twelve months earlier: Garrard, Ferguson and Little, with Garrard and Little the only veterans from the Fisher game in 2006. It showed how much of a rebuilding job Brown had done and it paid off, as the Dons made it to the final with a 3-1 win. The partnership of Cumbers and Main was flourishing up front, with Cumbers scoring the first and Main the next two as they progressed to a play-off final against Staines.

Luis Cumbers celebrates his equaliser in the play-off final against Staines Town, much to the disgust of Staines' players. (Newsquest)

Mark de Bolla roars with delight, having scored the free-kick that won AFC Wimbledon promotion. (Paul Willatts)

The squad celebrate their promotion out of the Isthmian League after four years. (Paul Willatts)

The match took place at Staines' Wheatsheaf Park, with three ex-Dons, Dave Sargent, Richard Butler and Lewis Cook, in the Staines squad. Terry Brown went with the same XI that had started against Hornchurch, but included de Bolla on the bench for the first time since he was sent out on loan.

Dons' James Pullen and Staines' James Courtnage both made outstanding saves early on, before Staines captain Matt Flitter – lucky not to be sent off for hauling Main down when he was through on goal – bundled in a corner to put Staines ahead. McDonnell came on for Finn at the break, but the Dons were struggling. With ten minutes left, it appeared they were set for more heartbreak, but fortune turned in their favour. Courtnage dropped a corner under pressure from Main and Cumbers threw himself at McDonnell's cross to level the scores. Staines were furious that no free-kick was given for Main's barge on Courtnage, but the goal stood.

Two minutes later, Wimbledon won a free-kick on the edge of box. Mark de Bolla, introduced with twenty minutes left for Ferguson, grabbed the ball and wrote himself into Wimbledon folklore by curling a beautiful free-kick into the bottom corner. It brought about mass hysteria among players and fans and, when Staines couldn't muster an equaliser, all that was left was for player of the year Goodliffe to lift the trophy.

At the third time of asking, Wimbledon were out of the Isthmian League and Brown had done what Anderson couldn't.

8

MAIN MAN

The Conference South may have been a step up the football ladder, but AFC Wimbledon took to it like a duck to water. Their record in the cups against Conference South teams gave them a confidence that proved justified as they finished top – just pipping old foes Hampton & Richmond to the title in a penultimate match showdown between the two.

The signing of Grays Athletic striker Danny Kedwell for £10,000 was a master stroke by Terry Brown, as Kedwell and Jon Main struck up a lethal partnership that scored fifty goals in league and cup games, with Main hitting thirty-four. They also helped propel Wimbledon to the FA Cup first round for the first time in their history.

Kingsmeadow continued to evolve into a ground capable of sustaining Wimbledon's success. The main stand was extended, and the Dons leased the land around the stadium from Kingstonian so they could make improvements, giving the Ks a new twenty-five-year lease to share the ground as part of the deal.

When it came to the playing staff, Brown showed a ruthless streak. Eight of his promotion-winning squad were released, including play-off final winner Mark de Bolla. Steve Ferguson and Rob Quinn, who had started the final, were shown the door, as were Mark Beard, Karl Beckford, Richard Jolly, Will Salmon and Daniel Webb. Robin Shroot's contract saga could not be figured out and he left to play for Harrow. In January, he was snapped up by Championship side Birmingham City in a deal that entitled Wimbledon to compensation as he was under twenty-four and they were his last contracted club. Marcus Gayle also decided to hang up his boots, but was soon back as the new reserve-team manager.

Brown needed reinforcements, and started by bringing back an old face in former Don Lewis Taylor, who had spent two seasons at Horsham since leaving Wimbledon. Unfortunately, he injured knee ligaments in pre-season and only returned for the final few games. Ben Judge signed for the season having been with the Dons since March, and defender Alan Inns and striker Elliott Godfrey both made the switch from Hampton. Midfielder Tom Davis joined from Lewes for a small fee and striker Chris Sullivan came from Braintree with a big reputation, but struggled to make an impact after a pre-season injury. Hendon striker Belal Aiteouakrim was snapped up, while youngster Kennedy Adjei was promoted from the reserves to the first team.

Pre-season was notable for Main's form, as he scored six goals, including a hat-trick in a 3-0 win over his old club Tonbridge Angels. The Supporters Direct Cup, meanwhile, was surrendered in a 2-1 defeat to Brentford.

Wimbledon announced their promotion credentials straight away in the season opener at Newport County. A 4-1 win sparked five straight victories and a nine-game unbeaten run that had them leading the table. Adjei, Judge, Inns, Davis and Godfrey all made their full debuts against a Newport side that had former Dons favourite Kevin Cooper in their team. But it was Main that stole the show, beginning the season as he meant to go on with a hat-trick. He followed that up with a goal in the 3-1 win over Bognor Regis Town and a late double as they beat Bromley 3-1; a match that saw Michael Haswell stretchered off with ankle ligament damage that kept him out for four months, after which he struggled to regain his place and fitness.

Vital to the Dons early season form was a stabilised team, with Brown starting just thirteen different players in the first eight games. Main was given the player of the month award for August and then got an extra present for the game against Maidstone United. Not only did he score two penalties in the 3-1 win, but he was joined up front in the second half by Kedwell, making his debut off the bench. It was the start of a beautiful partnership.

They started together for the first time in the next game, a top-of-the-table clash with Hayes & Yeading. Neither found the net in a 2-1 defeat though, which not only ended Wimbledon's unbeaten run, but also saw Hayes overtake them as league leaders. That first defeat was followed by a second as they lost 3-2 at Worcester City having been 3-0 down after twenty-four minutes.

But Wimbledon roared back with victories over Bishop's Stortford (4-1) and Havant & Waterlooville (3-0), with Main and Kedwell scoring six of their seven goals. They scored two more in the next game, but couldn't prevent a 3-2 defeat to fellow promotion hopefuls Chelmsford, who were the new leaders – eight points ahead of fourth-placed Wimbledon but having played three games more. Draws against Welling United (2-2) and Hampton (1-1) – the first time the Dons had taken a point off the Beavers – and a 2-0 defeat at Eastleigh, their worst performance of the season, did nothing to close that gap.

While Wimbledon's league form was slipping they had also gone out at the first hurdle in the Setanta League Cup, 1-0 to Chelmsford, and the London Senior Cup, 3-0 to Erith Town. The FA Cup though was providing all the excitement. Entering at the second qualifying round, they needed replays to get past Bedford Town, where Kedwell scored his first Wimbledon goal in a 3-0 win, and Dover Athletic, Kedwell again scoring in a 2-0 win where Tony Finn got the other goal. Isthmian Premier side Maidstone United were the only team standing between them and the first round, and the Dons grabbed the opportunity thanks to Sam Hatton's solitary goal giving them a 1-0 win. It earned Hatton the player of the round award and, like Rob Ursell and Byron Bubb in previous seasons, VIP tickets to the final.

Unsurprisingly, the media spotlight was back on Wimbledon as they prepared for their first appearance in the FA Cup first round proper – against League Two Wycombe Wanderers. Wycombe were the first Football League side the Dons had faced competitively, but they were unbeaten in their league, having only conceded six goals. It was the biggest game yet in the club's history and they repainted the dressing rooms, installed flags at the Tempest End and had to deal with a sixty-strong Setanta TV crew.

Fans flocked to the ground full of anticipation for the match on Monday 10 November, and the crowd of 4,528 was only thirty-two short of the 4,560 record that watched them beat Raynes Park Vale in the final game of their first season in 2003. Despite the superb

Luke Garrard talks to Setanta Sports after the FA Cup first-round defeat to Wycombe Wanderers, with Haydon the Womble listening in. (Newsquest)

atmosphere, Wycombe proved just too good, as Matt Harold scored a hat-trick to give them a 4-1 win. Hatton did give the Dons hope when his fifty-sixth-minute far-post finish made it 2-1, but there was to be no fairytale. Brown shouldered the blame and said he was naïve in setting his team up to play from the back, while Inns apologised to supporters for simple goals he and his defensive colleagues had conceded. The result and performance may not have been what Wimbledon had wanted, but they could take pride from a strong cup run that made up for a disappointing FA Trophy showing.

A 3-1 win over Worcester City in the final qualifying round, where Aiteouakrim scored his first Dons goals with a brace, set up a first-round match with Southern League side Uxbridge. Wimbledon, so used to providing cup shocks, were instead on the end of one themselves as they lost 2-1 and had Inns sent off. That, coupled with a 1-0 home defeat to Dulwich Hamlet in the Surrey Senior Cup, ended Wimbledon's cup participation for another year.

That left the league, and Wimbledon set off on a title surge, winning thirteen of the next fourteen games and taking forty-six points from a possible fifty-four in an eighteen-game unbeaten run that took them back to the top. Deadly duo Main and Kedwell were key to the run, scored twenty-nine goals between them. Main scored hat-tricks in the 3-0 win over Fisher Athletic on Boxing Day and the 5-1 win over Braintree, while Kedwell scored doubles in the 3-0 win over Newport and the 5-1 hammering of Bognor.

A new crowd record of 4,690 was set when the Dons hosted title rivals Chelmsford City on 31 January, having leapt above them to the top of the table on goal difference. Two Main goals brought about a 3-1 win and it was advantage Wimbledon. Four more wins put them nine points clear of Hampton, who were now second. Main took his goal tally to thirty in the 2-0 win over Worcester City that saw 'keeper Andy Little stretchered off with a ruptured cruciate knee ligament injury. He was the third Wimbledon player on the sidelines with the same injury, with Taylor having suffered it in pre-season and Luke Garrard in training in November. James Pullen was now the Dons' number one for the rest of the season.

Wimbledon went into the final seven games with a nine-point lead at the top and promotion looking a certainty. But, instead of cruising to the end, they made things interesting with back-to-back defeats to Welling United (1-0) and Eastleigh (2-1) that saw Hampton close the gap to three points with a game in hand and a match between the two to come at The Beveree. The Eastleigh defeat was a controversial one, with Tom Jordan punching their winner into the net and the officials failing to spot it. Inns' protests afterwards earned him a red card.

Wins against Team Bath (2-0) – thanks to goals from Kezie Ibe, signed on loan from Ebbsfleet, and Davis – and Basingstoke Town (1-0), through an Inns goal, recovered some composure that was blown away in another controversial game, this time at Bromley. Godfrey's early goal had been cancelled out by Ryan Hall, but Rocky Baptiste, signed by Brown to boost his strike force, bundled in an eighty-seventh-minute goal that put the Dons on the verge of the title. Deep into injury time, Main kicked the ball out to allow the stricken Jay Conroy, another player brought in by Brown, to receive treatment. When Bromley took

Jon Main scores one of his hat-trick goals against Braintree Town. The striker scored thirty-four goals to lead the Dons to the promotion. (Newsquest)

Elliott Godfrey takes a shot during the vital 3-1 over Chelmsford City that saw AFC Wimbledon open up a three-point gap at the top of the table that wouldn't be closed down. (Newsquest)

the throw in, Hall lofted the ball back to Pullen but hit it too hard, and lobbed the 'keeper for an equaliser that sparked angry scenes. Wimbledon wanted Bromley to stand back and let them score but, with Lilywhites manager Mark Goldberg not on the sidelines because of a knee injury, Derek Parnham was in charge and he refused, because Davis had allegedly thrown a water bottle at him. The match ended 2-2 with players and management squaring up to each other. Brown called Hall a 'typical idiot' and the Bromley bench a disgrace.

It meant Wimbledon went into their crunch match at Hampton three points clear of their opponents and with a much better goal difference, meaning a draw would give them the title bar a disastrous thirteen-goal swing in Hampton's favour on the last day. Having only taken one point from five meetings with Hampton, nerves were obviously on edge, even more so when Francis Quarm gave the Beavers the lead. They held off everything Wimbledon threw at them until three minutes before the end, when Main, on as a substitute, headed home Kedwell's cross and began jubilant celebrations that went long into the night in Wimbledon Village.

The final day party started with Judge being named Radio WDON player of the year, Main the Junior Dons player of the year, and Chris Hussey the young player of the year for the second season in a row. In front of a record 4,722 crowd, the Dons secured their first title in four years, with goals from Adjei, Hatton and Jason Goodliffe beating St Albans 3-0. Goodliffe lifted the trophy and it was a mission accomplished. Brown had delivered what he had promised two seasons ago – Conference football.

James Pullen shows his anger towards Bromley's management after their controversial equaliser in the 2-2 draw. (Paul Willatts)

Dons players get the promotion party started after their late draw at Hampton & Richmond. (Paul Willatts)

Captain Jason Goodliffe celebrates his goal in his final AFC Wimbledon appearance against St Albans, after which he lifted the Conference South trophy before retiring. (Newsquest)

9
MUCH PROMISE

Conference football was a whole different ball game for AFC Wimbledon. The league was peppered with full-time teams and sides willing to spend big to achieve a prized Football League spot. Promotion was always going to be a struggle for the Dons but they gave it a good go, sitting in the top five for most of the first half of the season before a dreadful second half saw them slip away. An eighth-place finish was not to be sniffed at though, and there was another appearance in the first round of the FA Cup and a run to the London Senior Cup final.

There was sadness too, as Allen Batsford, the man who had managed Wimbledon FC to three successive Southern League titles in the 1970s and got them into the Football League for the first time, collapsed and passed away on his way home from watching Chelsea play Fulham in December. He had been in the Kingsmeadow stands watching the Dons beat Hayes & Yeading just two days earlier. It was the second death to affect the club in a month, after former reserve-team manager John Morris lost his battle with lung cancer.

On the playing front, Brown again showed no mercy, by cutting nine of his Conference South winners and seeing Jason Goodliffe retire. Tony Finn and Tom Davis were all part of the squad that played Hampton & Richmond in the title decider, but were let go. Belal Aiteouakirm, Jake Leberl, Andy Sambrook and Chris Sullivan were the other main names to depart, while fringe players Dean Mason and Luke Pigden also left.

Replacing them were Hayes & Yeading midfielder Steven Gregory, Ebbsfleet players Luke Moore and Derek Duncan, Ashford Town (Middlesex) midfielder Ricky Wellard and defender Brett Johnson, who had played in the Football League for Brentford. There was also a return for Paul Lorraine, who had spent two seasons at Woking, but was enticed back with Brown and the club putting plans in place to go full-time, which they did the following season.

With Andy Little still out injured, a new goalkeeper was required as back up to James Pullen and, after impressing in the friendlies, teenager Seb Brown was signed. Brown was a Wimbledon fan and had followed their struggles and formation as a child, often supporting from the terraces. Little recovered before Christmas, but was released and moved to Croydon Athletic. His fellow knee ligament victim Luke Garrard earned a new deal but found himself down the pecking order and joined Boreham Wood in February, ending a four-year association with the Dons.

The Supporters Direct Cup returned to Wimbledon once more, with Ben Judge and youngster Peter Rapson scoring in a 2-0 win over FC United in a pre-season that also included victory against a Fulham XI, with trialist Calum Willock scoring before a move for the striker broke down the next day.

The opening game of the season could not have been more appetising: a home match against Luton Town, relegated from League Two the season before and managed by Mick Harford, who played eighty-two times for Wimbledon between 1994 and 1998. Considering the Hatters had been playing two tiers above Wimbledon just three months earlier, a 1-1 draw was a more than credible result for Brown's men. Lorraine, Johnson, Gregory and Duncan all made full debuts, while Wellard and Moore came off the bench in a game of two penalties, with Wimbledon's scored by Jon Main. It was the first time they had not won their first game of the season.

Despite seeing that result followed by a 1-0 loss at Eastbourne Borough, Wimbledon acclimatised to their new surroundings in impressive fashion, losing only two of their first thirteen league games. Danny Kedwell and Moore both scored twice in a 4-0 win against Salisbury, but a Jay Conroy own goal and Kedwell penalty miss meant a 1-0 defeat to undefeated league leaders Oxford United. Barring the spot-kick miss, Kedwell was in fine form, scoring ten goals in the thirteen games, while Main had three, all of which came from the penalty spot. It had been a good run of results and had the Dons in fourth after a 1-0 win over Rushden & Diamonds that saw Terry Brown sent to the stands, despite an early winner from Ross Montague, a twenty-year-old midfielder signed from Brentford.

Their form took an unexpected dip as they took just four points from six games, with three home defeats in a row and a 3-1 loss at Chester City, a result later expunged from the records when Chester went out of business. One plus point was Main's first goals from open play in the 5-2 win over Forest Green Rovers. He scored a brace in a match that was 3-2 after just twenty-three minutes.

Chris Hussey's performances, meanwhile, had caught the eye of Championship club Coventry City, and they snapped up the twenty-year-old left-back on loan before buying him permanently in January. His success was testament to the Dons youth system, and he made his goodbyes with a parade around the pitch before a 2-1 defeat to Kettering. The Dons also lost defender Alan Inns to a cruciate knee ligament injury that ruled him out for the season. The same injury ended Montague's campaign in January.

Hussey's departure meant he missed the FA Cup exploits and another big first-round draw. Being a Conference club meant the Dons entered the competition at the fourth qualifying round, where they faced fellow Conference side Crawley Town, who they had already drawn 1-1 with in the league. Sam Hatton's low drive just before half-time resulted in the same scoreline in the cup and a replay at Kingsmeadow, which the Dons won 3-1 with goals from Main, Moore and Kedwell, despite Duncan's red card for a second booking in first-half injury time. It meant a trip to League One Millwall.

Once more, the build-up produced much excitement but the Dons could not instigate the cup upset they hoped for. They did keep the score goalless for forty-nine minutes before Neil Harris put the Lions ahead and Jason Price doubled the lead. Lewis Taylor pulled a goal back after being played in by Kedwell's back heel, but a goal from Danny Schofield and another from Price gave Millwall a 4-1 win and ended Wimbledon's FA Cup dream for another season.

Elliott Godfrey challenges for the ball during the first game of AFC Wimbledon's Conference season against Luton Town. (Newsquest)

With Pullen ruled out for a month with a chipped bone in his ankle, Seb Brown was given his chance in goal and took it, by helping the Dons to five straight wins and winning the player of the month award for December for keeping six clean sheets in a row. Main moved into double figures with a double in the 2-0 win over Salisbury, which he followed with another two goals in the 5-0 trouncing of Hayes & Yeading on Boxing Day that moved the Dons into fourth.

When Hayes avenged their defeat with a 1-0 win a week later, Terry Brown acted by delving into the transfer market. Striker Nathan Elder, on loan from Shrewsbury Town, winger Glenn Poole and left-back Danny Blanchett, on loan from Peterborough United, all arrived in time for a 2-0 win over Mansfield Town that saw Elder score inside two minutes. It was Wimbledon's first victory of the season against a top-five side.

The FA Trophy promised success, but ended with a shock exit with the Dons on the verge of making the quarter-finals for the first time. Having entered at the first round proper, goals from Kedwell and Luis Cumbers, who had returned on loan from Gillingham, dispatched Isthmian Premier Division side Boreham Wood 2-1, and then Wellard, Main and Judge strikes defeated fellow Conference side Altrincham 3-1. That meant they were in the third round, equalling the furthest they had got in the competition, and facing

Workington from Conference North. It was an excellent opportunity to make the last eight, but despite Elder and Kedwell twice putting Wimbledon ahead, two goals in the last ten minutes from Jonny Wright and Shaun Vipond gave Workington a 3-2 cup upset.

It was a disappointing defeat that epitomised what was to come in the league, as Wimbledon finished with a whimper and failed to record back-to-back victories. When they could only draw 2-2 at ten-man Cambridge United, a side that had lost their past seven games, it left the Dons eighth, five points behind Luton. The Hatters were next up in a game that did provide some cheer, as Wimbledon went to Kenilworth Road and recorded a great 2-1 win, with Elder and Kedwell the goalscorers once more.

After three games without victory and Taylor seeing his season ended by another cruciate ligament injury, this time in the opposite knee to the one the season before, a 2-0 win at Eastbourne Borough meant Wimbledon were still in touch with the play-offs. With ten games to go, they were two points behind fifth with a game in hand.

But in the story of their season, it proved too much of an ask, and they lost seven of their final ten matches, taking just seven points. Among those results was a dramatic 2-2 draw with Wrexham. Kedwell missed a first-half penalty before Pullen and Frank Sinclair scored own goals for the game to enter injury time at 1-1. Andy Mangan put Wrexham ahead to seemingly claim victory, until Sinclair punched Kedwell at a corner, was sent off and conceded a penalty that Poole scored for an equaliser. A 3-1 loss to champions-elect Stevenage Borough and a 5-0 thrashing at York City mathematically meant the play-offs were out of reach with four games to go.

While the chances of a third successive promotion were slipping away, Wimbledon made the last four of both the Surrey Senior Cup and London Senior Cup, both of which had their fair share of drama. After Ash United were swatted away 7-1 in the second round of the Surrey Cup, Duncan's late equaliser secured a 1-1 draw with Camberley Town in the third round that was settled 6-5 on penalties. It put Wimbledon into the quarter-finals where they almost suffered a shock defeat. Despite fielding their first team at Isthmian Division One South Chipstead, they were losing 3-2 with a minute left before Gregory equalised and Poole won it in injury time. With the semi-final against Godalming Town the day after the York game, the Dons had to field a young team that lost 2-0 and missed out on a third final appearance.

In the London competition, Wimbledon started with an abandoned game at Tooting & Mitcham, where the referee ended proceedings after seventy minutes with the Dons trailing 1-0 as sections of the Imperial Fields pitch were frozen. The rearranged match a week later ended 2-2 with Main scoring twice and had to be settled by penalties that ended 4-3 to Wimbledon. Next up was Harrow Borough in the quarter-final, and youngster Matt Harmsworth took centre stage with a double in a 3-2 win to set up a last four tie with Croydon Athletic. The Rams were fighting for promotion from Isthmian Division One South so fielded a young side, while the Dons, with nothing else to play for, played their first team and won 3-0 with Elder, Will Hendry, signed earlier in the season from Maidenhead United, and youngster Ryan Jackson all scoring to set up a final with Met Police.

To prepare for the final, Wimbledon limped to an eighth-place league finish, fourteen points off the play-offs, as they lost three of their final four games. The only bright spot

Steven Gregory shows his teammates something interesting after scoring against Gateshead. (Newsquest)

was a 1-0 win over Mansfield, thanks to Kedwell's goal and two late Seb Brown penalty saves. Kedwell ended the season with twenty-six goals and swept the board at the player awards, winning the Allen Batsford WISA player of the year, players' player of the year, Junior Dons player of the year and Radio WDON player of the year. Seb Brown won the young payer of the year award.

A final day 1-0 defeat at Gateshead came four days before the cup final, with Isthmian Division One South Met Police at Harrow Borough. The Dons were overwhelming favourites, but defended poorly to draw 4-4 after extra time and lose 4-3 on penalties. Kedwell, Moore and a Godfrey penalty had Wimbledon 3-1 up and coasting, but Gary Drewett pulled a goal back and Vernon Francis equalised with five minutes left to bring about extra time. Wellard's finish in the 116th minute should have been the end of matters, but once more they could not hold out and Steve Sutherland's goal meant penalties. Moore, Judge and Kedwell all scored but Jack Stafford and Godfrey missed, leaving Paul Honey to secure the Police's triumph and leave Wimbledon to end the season without a trophy for the first time under Brown.

Danny Kedwell goes close against Workington, but could not prevent a shock 3-2 defeat in the FA Trophy. (Newsquest)

Jon Main reflects on his missed penalty against Barrow as his and AFC Wimbledon's form slumped. (Newsquest)

Danny Kedwell accepts the WISA Allen Batsford player of the year trophy from Maureen Batsford, wife of the late legendary Wimbledon manager. (Newsquest)

10

PROMOTION CHARGE

If the first season in the Conference Premier ended disappointingly for AFC Wimbledon, then their second campaign finished much better. They hit the league with renewed vigour, spending large parts of it at the top before being overhauled by Crawley. They did cement a play-off place though, while the possibility of meeting MK Dons in the FA Cup – a prospect feared by Wimbledon fans, but eagerly anticipated elsewhere in the football world – almost became a reality as Wimbledon made it to the second round for the first time.

There was also a decision on the future direction of the club, instigated by events with Darragh MacAnthony in 2006 and impatience among Wimbledon fans for a move back to Merton. An independent survey was launched by the Dons Trust that asked Dons Trust members, season-ticket holders and casual fans how they would like the club to proceed. Six options ranged from staying in Kingston, to moving to Merton or selling the club to a rich owner who could fast-track them into the Premier League. The results confirmed what many already believed, with over a third wanting to keep the club fan-owned while they found a small ground in Wimbledon with expansion potential. Given what the supporters had gone through in 2002, it was no surprise that only nine people out of 730 wanted the club sold to a rich owner.

The playing staff underwent another massive shake-up, with Terry Brown searching for a squad capable of fighting for promotion and fulfilling the demands of going full-time. Out went Jay Conroy, Derek Duncan, Elliott Godfrey, Will Hendry, Ben Judge, Paul Lorraine, Glenn Poole, James Pullen and Peter Rapson. Long-term injury victims Ross Montague, Alan Inns and Lewis Taylor were also shown the door. Kennedy Adjei was loaned to Sutton United, while young 'keeper Jack Turner was now Seb Brown's understudy in goal.

In came striker Christian Jolley from Kingstonian, midfielder Lee Minshull from Tonbridge Angels, left-back Andre Blackman, striker Mark Nwokeji, midfielder Rashid Yussuff from Gillingham and defender Ismail Yakubu from Barnet. Trialists Sammy Moore, Ed Harris, Fraser Franks, Reece Jones and Delano Sam-Yorke all did enough during pre-season, which included a 2-1 win over an Arsenal XI featuring Ryo Miyaichi and Benik Afobe, to earn deals.

Having won eight of their ten pre-season games and held onto captain Danny Kedwell despite the best efforts of Crawley Town to pry him away, Wimbledon were feeling confident when they opened their campaign on 14 August. It proved justified as they beat

Southport 1-0 and won their first three games without conceding a goal, Brown naming the same starting line-up for every match. Blackman, Sammy Moore and Yakubu made debuts against Southport and Jolley came off the bench to score the winner after Jon Main had a penalty saved. Minshull also debuted off the bench, but was sent off for a heavy challenge just six minutes after coming on.

A 1-0 defeat at Rushden & Diamonds was the only blemish in their first eight games, in which Kedwell hit eight goals as they went top of the league, and there was international recognition for Sam Hatton, Seb Brown and Steven Gregory. They were called up to the England C squad for a 2-2 draw with Wales and would play for their country several times during the campaign.

A first big test for Wimbledon came when they faced back-to-back games against promotion rivals Luton Town and Crawley in September. Luton avenged their defeat at Kenilworth Road the previous season by beating the Dons 3-0, but there was joy against Crawley with Kedwell scoring the winner, against the side that had tried to buy him in the summer, in a 2-1 win. Hatton, now playing at right-back, scored the first. They continued to trade top spot with Crawley, as a run of thirteen points from five games in early October failed to pull them clear. Sammy Moore scored after just eleven seconds in the 5-2 win at Mansfield Town, and Jolley hit four goals in as many matches. But almost every time they did go top, Wimbledon would lose their next match and Crawley would go back to the summit.

For the third season in a row, Wimbledon made the first round proper of the FA Cup by beating Basingstoke Town 1-0 thanks to Harris's first senior goal. It set up a tie with Conference South side Ebbsfleet and a big chance to make the second round for the first time. A 0-0 draw at home, where Jolley was sent off thirty-eight minutes in for a two-footed tackle, meant a replay. But before that could be played, the draw threw up a potentially nightmare scenario. If Wimbledon got past Ebbsfleet they would face MK Dons at Kingsmeadow, if they too won a replay against Stevenage. The draw made national headlines, with some sections of the football world eager to see the grudge match take place, while Wimbledon's fans had no intention of recognising the existence of the other club. Wimbledon themselves kept it professional and released a simple statement.

> Most people know the way that Milton Keynes obtained their football club. It was wrong then and it is still wrong now, which makes this fixture very painful for us.
>
> However, when we entered the FA Cup we understood that this might happen and we will go about our business professionally and complete the fixture. But we would have preferred that it hadn't happened.

In the end, there was nothing to worry about, as Milton Keynes lost their replay at Stevenage 7-6 on penalties. Seb Brown admitted that the players were relieved to have avoided the media circus. Wimbledon played their replay two days later, but still almost blew their chance of progression. Sammy Moore, fast becoming a fans' favourite, had to equalise with the last kick of normal time for a 2-2 draw and then score a last-minute winner in extra time. His heroics meant a debut match in the second round with Stevenage, winners of the Conference the previous season. It was a chance to make the third round and get a Premier

Sammy Moore became a big hit with fans after his pre-season signing, and here celebrates his opening goal against Tamworth. (Newsquest)

League side to Kingsmeadow. But Stevenage proved too strong in front of the television cameras, winning 2-0 with Wimbledon's Harris sent off for two bookings.

The end of 2010 was disrupted by heavy snow, but the Dons ended it on top after a 3-0 win over Eastbourne, with Nwokeji, Wellard and Yussuff all scoring to give them a three-point lead.

Brown shuffled his pack once more by bringing in Kirk Hudson and James Mulley to provide the goals from midfield he felt were lacking. Mulley did just that by scoring on his New Year's Day debut, a 3-1 win over Hayes & Yeading, and again two days later in a 3-3 draw at Newport County. Experienced defender Jamie Stuart came in from Rushden and left-back Gareth Gwillim from Dagenham & Redbridge, with Blackman leaving and Chris Bush recalled by Brentford after a loan spell. Main had been struggling for goals – he had just one in the London Senior Cup – and went on loan to Dartford.

Wimbledon's Trophy exploits ended in the second round with defeat to Conference South Woking. Having beaten Braintree Town in the first round 3-0 with goals from Nwokeji, Jolley and Kedwell, the Dons suffered an exit at a club below them in the league pyramid for the third successive year, losing 3-2 having twice come from behind. That was followed by a 2-1 loss to Colliers Wood United at the first hurdle in the Surrey Senior Cup.

There was almost joy in the London Senior Cup as they made it to the semi-finals. An injury-time Main goal had beaten Dulwich Hamlet 3-2 earlier in the season, while youngster Harry Knock proved the hero in a last-minute extra-time 4-3 win over Beckenham Town in the quarter-finals. They were on course for a chance to make amends for their defeat in the final last season but, despite fielding a strong side and coming back from 2-0 down against Isthmian Premier League side Hendon, an extra-time Dave Diedhiou winner put them out and ended cup hopes for the season.

That left the league and – despite inconsistent form that saw Wimbledon not win away for two and a half months before a 2-0 win at Gateshead at the end of January – they were still ten games unbeaten and sitting on top of the pile. An eleventh game in thirty-two days proved too much as they lost 4-1 at York City, but three wins in a row, including a 1-0 victory over York in the reverse fixture, had them four points clear but having played five games more than Crawley.

Drewe Broughton's signing-on loan from Lincoln in February caused dissension in the Wimbledon ranks. The striker had played thirteen games for MK Dons in 2007 and was the first player AFC Wimbledon had signed that had also turned out for their Milton Keynes rivals. Many fans did not want any players to sign for Wimbledon who had played for the other club, but realised that would become increasingly impossible as time went on. Broughton himself went some way to winning over the fans by scoring on his debut in the 5-2 win against Tamworth, and then again in the 4-1 defeat of Altrincham where Kedwell hit a hat-trick.

As the season entered the final stretch, Wimbledon handed the title to Crawley by taking one point from four games in early March. After 2-1 defeats to Grimsby and Kidderminster Harriers, in which Sammy Moore dislocated his knee and was ruled out for the season, the Dons travelled to their title rivals. If they were to stay in touch then nothing but a win would do. They didn't get it though, as they lost 3-1, despite the home side having Dannie Bulman sent off in the first half. Terry Brown as good as conceded the title and was now looking over his shoulder at Luton, Wrexham, York, Kidderminster and Fleetwood, who all wanted their play-off spot.

He was wary of last season's poor finish and, to counter it, signed striker Kaid Mohamed from Bath City. On his debut against Rushden, he earned the penalty that Kedwell scored for a 1-0 win that began a fantastic run of form of six wins and one draw in Wimbledon's final seven matches to clinch second. Kedwell and Luke Moore scored twice each in a 4-0 win at relegated Histon that guaranteed a top-three finish and a home second leg in the play-off semi-final, while the 0-0 Easter Monday draw at Forest Green Rovers secured the runners-up spot.

With excitement for the play-offs building, there was still time for a sad goodbye to Main. The striker had spent the second half of the season on loan at Dartford and Dover Athletic, but came back in time for the final home against Grimsby, already knowing his contract was not being renewed. He came on for the final twenty-five minutes but, despite his teammates' best efforts to set him up, there was to be no fairytale goal, in a 2-1 win that saw the Dons end the season fifteen points behind champions Crawley. Main finished his four-year stay with sixty-one goals in 118 appearances.

Sam Hatton was named WISA Allen Batsford player of the year, while Seb Brown claimed the Radio WDON player of the year, Junior Dons player of the year and the young player of the year awards. They would have swapped them all for play-off glory.

Danny Kedwell refused a transfer to Crawley Town in the summer of 2010 and then scored this winner against them, bending the ball beyond 'keeper Nick Jordan. (Newsquest)

Josh Walker scores Stevenage's first goal from a free-kick as Wimbledon were outclassed in their first appearance in the FA Cup second round, but they had avoided a tie with rivals MK Dons. (Newsquest)

Drewe Broughton's signing in February caused a stir after his past playing for MK Dons. He won over Wimbledon fans though, with goals in his first two appearances, including this one against Altrincham. (Newsquest)

11

IT ONLY TOOK NINE YEARS

AFC Wimbledon had to wait six days before they began their play-off campaign for a spot in the Football League. Despite finishing second, they were not favourites to go up, with third-placed Luton Town, who played Wrexham in the other semi-final, given the bookies' backing. They were, however, favourites for their two-legged semi-final against Fleetwood Town, who had finished fifth, twelve points behind the Dons, and who Wimbledon had drawn 1-1 with and beaten 1-0 during the regular season.

The first leg was on a Friday night, 6 May, at Fleetwood's Highbury ground. Not often do the away sides come away with comfortable wins in the play-offs, but that was exactly what Wimbledon did, as Luke Moore and Kaid Mohamed scored in a 2-0 win. Moore scored when he ran on to Sean Gregan's underhit back-pass and kept his cool to slide home the opener. He then set up Mohamed to double the lead before half-time, latching on to Ricky Wellard's throughball and squaring for the striker to clip into the corner. The entire tie could have been settled that night, but Danny Kedwell, Brett Johnson and Rashid Yussuff all missed chances. Seb Brown only had to make one decent save from Junior Brown to send Wimbledon into the return leg at Kingsmeadow five days later in a strong position.

It was one of the famous Kingsmeadow nights as Wimbledon, brimming with confidence and quality, ended the semi-final as a contest by scoring inside a minute to set up a 6-1 thrashing and an 8-1 aggregate win.

Mohamed settled any nerves by speeding past Gregan and slotting under Danny Hurst almost straight from the kick-off, and by half-time Fleetwood may as well have got on the coach home. Kedwell scored his twenty-sixth of the season when he converted Sam Hatton's diagonal ball, and Moore again set up Mohamed to tap into an empty net and take the aggregate score to 5-1 with forty-five minutes still to play.

Fleetwood salvaged some pride when Gareth Sneddon scored after half-time, but Wimbledon stepped up a gear again and scored three more. Mohamed had his hat-trick when he converted the rebound after Steven Gregory hit the post, and Christian Jolley capitalised on more woeful defending to add a fifth goal. The Dons still weren't done until James Mulley scored the goal of the bunch with ten minutes left. Having won the ball in his own box, he raced past two Fleetwood players, played a one-two with Yussuff and then rounded Hurst to slot into an empty net. On this form, nothing looked like stopping Wimbledon.

Standing in their way though were Luton, who beat Wrexham 3-0 in their first leg and 2-1 in the second for their own impressive 5-1 aggregate score. After two years in the Conference, Luton were impatient and wanted their place back in the Football League.

Kaid Mohamed was Wimbledon's main man in the play-off semi-final against Fleetwood Town, scoring four of their eight goals over two legs and a hat-trick in the second leg. (Newsquest)

They had also taken four points and not conceded a goal against Wimbledon in their two meetings that season.

A ten-day gap between the semi-final and the final meant a nervous wait for Wimbledon fans while the build-up in the press reached fever pitch. The national media descending on the Dons' New Malden training ground, fascinated by the fairytale nature of their rise through non-League football. Terry Brown, Erik Samuelson and Kedwell were all under the media spotlight but took it all in their stride, concentrating only on the matter in hand. For Brown, he was hoping for third time lucky having twice led Aldershot to the play-off final but lost both times on penalties.

On 21 May, nearly 7,000 Dons fans made the journey up to Manchester – the final was there due to a clash with the Champions League final at Wembley. They were nervous, excited and ready to party. Brown's line-up was predictable – he had said in the media his team would be unchanged from the semi-finals. Seb Brown was in goal; Hatton, Johnson, Jamie Stuart and Gareth Gwillim in defence; Gregory in the holding midfield role; Wellard and Yussuff in midfield; and Moore playing just behind Kedwell and Mohamed.

After a cagey opening in a boisterous and loud atmosphere, the Dons thought they were ahead when Mohamed forced a good save out of Mark Tyler and Kedwell put the rebound into an empty net. His, and the fans, celebrations were cut short by the linesman's correctly judged offside flag. Seb Brown made three big saves to keep Luton out before Gwillim and Wellard had to go off with injuries just after the hour mark, with Ismail Yakubu and Mulley replacing them.

James Mulley rounds off the scoring against Fleetwood Town with the best goal of the semi-final. (Newsquest)

Mulley's introduction brought the Dons to life, but it wasn't until injury time that the real drama began. Jack Howell's cross found Jason Walker at the back post and his header back across goal looked a certain match-winner. The crowd held their breath and gasped as the ball somehow hit the post and rebounded straight into Seb Brown's grateful arms. Most of the supporters, players and management had thought it was in, but Wimbledon survived.

The deadlock meant extra time, where Gregory, also struggling with injury, made way for Lee Minshull. Much like the normal ninety minutes, the real action came at the end of the extra period with a frantic final five minutes in which the Dons twice thought they had won it. First, Moore found Mohamed in the box and the in-form striker struck the outside of the post when he looked odds on to score. Then, with almost the last action of the game, Yakubu really should have sent Wimbledon fans into ecstasy. Hatton was given time to cross from the right and he found the big defender at the back post. With the whole goal to aim at, Yakubu got his jump all wrong, got under the ball and headed it over. It was a horrendous miss. Terry Brown threw his water bottle in the air in disgust and soon the final whistle signalled the lottery of penalties, his worst nightmare.

The Dons had been practising for this eventuality since losing to Crawley in March, and got off to the perfect start when Seb Brown, the boyhood AFC Wimbledon fan, saved Alex Lawless's opening kick. Hatton fired his high into the net to make it advantage Dons.

Moore kept the Dons ahead by keeping his nerve after George Pilkington had scored for Luton, but they were pegged back when Mohamed's weak effort was saved by Tyler. With Adam Newton netting his penalty, the scores were level again.

With the pendulum swinging back in Luton's favour, Seb Brown produced another moment of heroism when he brilliantly stuck up a left hand when on the ground to claw away Walker's chipped spot-kick. Yakubu showed courage to put his earlier miss behind

Wimbledon fans link together as they prepare for the lottery of penalties. (Newsquest)

him and stroke home his penalty, putting Wimbledon back in the driving seat. Howells had to score to keep the tie alive and did just that to put all the pressure on Dons captain Kedwell.

Kedwell had been inspirational throughout the season but this was a pressure kick – score and the Dons were in the Football League. The outcome was never in doubt. Kedwell kept his cool, took his time and hammered his kick full pelt into the net – no 'keeper could have saved it.

Pandemonium ensued. Wimbledon players, management and supporters erupted in disbelief. Heroes Kedwell and Brown were engulfed by team mates and supporters who broke on to the pitch, while the Luton squad collapsed in heartbreak.

Kedwell recovered his composure and led his side up the steps to lift the play-off trophy, sparking even more wild scenes of celebration back on the pitch below. Terry Brown's emotions were even getting the better of him, as he smashed home an imaginary penalty from the same spot from which Wimbledon achieved the goal that meant so much to so many. The celebrations went long into the night and Manchester was turned yellow and blue by players and fans alike.

The next day, the heroic squad returned to a jubilant welcome and party at Kingsmeadow, parading the trophy around the stadium in front of their applauding fans and once more drinking well into the night. The celebrations did not stop there and one unnamed fan was so happy he paid for all the players to jet off to Las Vegas!

After three promotions in four years under Brown, and five in total, AFC Wimbledon's tenure in non-League football was over.

It only took nine years.

Seb Brown sticks up a strong left hand to keep out Jason Walker's penalty in the shoot-out – his second save from four penalties to put Wimbledon on the brink of promotion. (Newsquest)

Danny Kedwell starts the celebrations after slamming home the penalty that put AFC Wimbledon into the Football League for the first time. (Newsquest)

Captain Kedwell lifts the play-off trophy surrounded by teammates. (Newsquest)

The champagne flows as players, management and their families celebrate the historic promotion. (Paul Willatts)

Terry Brown finally gets his hands on the play-off trophy after two final defeats when in charge of Aldershot Town. (Newsquest)

Penalty hero Seb Brown is welcomed back to Kingsmeadow by jubilant AFC Wimbledon fans. (Newsquest)

Terry Brown (left) and chief executive Erik Samuelson (right) hold the play-off trophy, surrounded by coaches and players at a civic reception held by Merton Council. (Newsquest)

12

BACK IN THE BIG TIME

Excitement was, quite naturally, at a peak as AFC Wimbledon returned to the Football League. The party atmosphere from Manchester lasted through the summer and for the first two months of the season, as the Dons lived up to pre-season talk of back-to-back promotions by challenging at the very top of League Two. But a woeful slump from October onwards saw them flirt with the relegation places and, by the end of the season, some fans were even questioning whether Terry Brown was the right man at the helm.

Promotion had sparked a hectic summer of work to upgrade Kingsmeadow to Football League standards. New CCTV was needed covering the whole ground, new showers in the changing rooms and new dugouts had to be installed and plans put in place to increase the seating capacity.

While the stadium needed changing, Brown tried his best to keep his promotion-winning squad together. Instead of orchestrating a massive overhaul, he wanted to give the players that had got Wimbledon into the Football League the chance to play for them in it. On top of Jon Main's release, four others were shown the exit door, the most surprising of which was Ismail Yakubu. Fringe players Ed Harris, Mark Nwokeji and Delano Sam-Yorke were also let go.

The problem with success is that it attracts attention, and Wimbledon were about to lose two of their best players. Captain and star striker Danny Kedwell sent shockwaves through the club by handing in a transfer request after the players returned from Las Vegas. Wimbledon tried their best to change his mind, but Kedwell was insistent and they reluctantly accepted. It was Gillingham that had stolen Kedwell's heart. As his home-town club he could not resist their lure and left the Dons, insisting the Gulls were the only team he would ever have departed for. As final acts go, his promotion-winning penalty kick in Manchester wasn't a bad way to bow out. Steven Gregory had also caught the eye of League One Bournemouth. The Cherries had an initial bid for the midfielder rejected but returned a week later and a deal was struck. Brown had suddenly lost two of his biggest players.

Kaid Mohamed chose Cheltenham Town over a permanent move to Wimbledon, leaving Brown desperate for a new striking hero, but luckily he already had one lined up. Jack Midson, a free agent since his release from Oxford United, had already agreed to join the Dons before Kedwell's departure but only officially signed after. He was to become the next Dons star.

Also moving to Wimbledon were fellow striker Charles Ademeno from Grimsby Town, midfielder Max Porter from Rushden & Diamonds and left-back Chris Bush, on loan at

Wimbledon for a period last season, while Gareth Gwillim's loan from Dagenham was turned permanent. Defender Mat Mitchel-King signed from Crewe Alexandra, but was diagnosed with glandular fever in pre-season and missed the first half of the campaign, getting injured when he recovered.

The feel-good factor continued to reverberate around Kingsmeadow when they beat a Fulham XI 2-0 with goals from Brett Johnson and Ademeno to start a decent pre-season that included a 2-1 win over a strong Watford side. There was also a shoot-out win over a Bedfont Town side managed by former Dons striker Kevin Cooper, in a match played in memory of Wimbledon's former reserve-team manager John Morris.

The competitive season started early as Wimbledon were forced to play a preliminary-round League Cup match with familiar foes Crawley Town. Birmingham City's victory in the cup, and subsequent Premier League relegation the season before, meant they were seeded through to the third round and one less team was needed in the first round. Having just come up, Wimbledon and Crawley were the two lowest-ranked teams in the Football League and therefore chosen to face off in a preliminary-round tie at Crawley's Broadfield Stadium on 29 July. Neither team was happy about the situation, as it robbed them of a week of pre-season and the chance to play a Football League big boy, although they knew the winner would then play Crystal Palace. That was to be Crawley, who won 3-2, despite Luke Moore and Midson twice giving the Dons the lead. Three defensive errors gave the Reds victory. Midson and Porter were given full debuts while Bush and Ademeno came off the bench.

Thoughts then turned to the League campaign and an opening match at home to Bristol Rovers, relegated from League One the season before and one of the favourites to go up. Once more the media were in a spin about Wimbledon's miraculous journey, and players and management were swamped by cameras and journalists from all over the country. Again they dealt with the attention well, with Erik Samuelson talking about the start of a new journey for AFC Wimbledon. He also admitted to being quietly confident of at least a shot at the play-offs.

Wimbledon wore replica white shirts from Wimbledon FC's first league game against Halifax Town in 1977 in a match that was a tidal wave of emotions in front of a sell-out 4,629 crowd – their third biggest. Those supporters were in shock after twenty minutes though, as Rovers went 2-0 up, taking advantage of two more Dons defensive errors. New captain Jamie Stuart glanced Sam Hatton's free-kick in on the stroke of half-time to spark renewed hope, and they got a deserved equaliser on sixty-nine minutes, Ademeno firing home on the turn from Lee Minshull's knock down. Once more they imploded at the back though, and Johnson handled a cross to give Adam Virgo the chance to score from the spot. He did just that and handed the Dons their first-ever opening-day defeat, 3-2.

Wimbledon had conceded six easy goals in two games, but they learned quickly, and seven wins in their next eleven matches had everyone smiling again. Midson found his feet with a double in a 2-0 win at Plymouth Argyle as he and Christian Jolley formed a superb partnership. The latter, having only been included on the bench when Ademeno was injured in the warm up, scored a sublime injury-time winner in the 3-2 victory over Port Vale that even had Terry Brown doing his best Jose Mourinho impression down the touchline.

Sitting fifteenth after seven games, Wimbledon lifted themselves to third with four straight wins. Midson and Jolley were rampant, scoring eight goals between them in wins over Cheltenham Town (4-1), Bradford City (2-1), Gillingham (3-1) on Kedwell's Kingsmeadow return, and Morecambe (2-1). If other results had gone their way, Wimbledon could have been top of the pile after the Morecambe win, but instead had to settle for a place in the automatic places.

The good League form was transferred to the first round of the Football League Trophy where they faced Stevenage, now a League One side after successive promotions, in the second round at Kingsmeadow. Stevenage had former Don Robin Shroot in their side but, despite fielding a number of fringe players, it was Wimbledon who went through 4-3 on penalties after a 2-2 draw. Jack Turner was the hero with two penalty saves. Their spot-kick luck ran out in the next round as a 1-1 draw at Swindon Town was followed by a 3-1 shoot-out defeat.

Captain Jamie Stuart (far left) heads home AFC Wimbledon's first goal in the Football League against Bristol Rovers. (Paul Willatts)

Charles Ademeno, in replica kit from Wimbledon's debut in the Football League in 1977, wheels away after scoring the equaliser against Bristol Rovers, converting Lee Minshull's (also pictured) knock-down. (Paul Willatts)

By the time they played Swindon, Wimbledon's League form had taken a severe turn for the worse. They were in the midst of a twelve-match winless run that lasted for two months until January. A 5-2 defeat at home to Crawley in October saw them slip out of the play-off places not to return. There was a 4-0 loss at Torquay and six straight defeats over the Christmas and New Year programme, albeit mostly against teams vying for promotion, had fans grumbling and players speaking out in support of Terry Brown.

In the midst of their poor run, Wimbledon did manage a shock in the FA Cup, putting out League One Scunthorpe United 1-0 in a replay after a 0-0 draw at Kingsmeadow. Luke Moore scored the vital winner that at least raised a little cheer. They had the chance for the second year running to make the third round for the first time, but stumbled out of the competition at Bradford, who were below them in the League. Midson was still scoring goals and got one but could not prevent a disappointing 3-1 defeat.

The Surrey Senior Cup and London Senior Cup were now primarily used to blood youngsters and give fringe players a game. A 2-1 defeat at Corinthian Casuals ended their

Surrey Cup participation at the second round, but there was another run to the last four of the London Cup. Wins against Wingate & Finchley (2-1) and Met Police (5-0) put them in the semi-finals and set up another tie with Hendon, who they had lost to at the same stage the season before. It was a chance for revenge, but history repeated itself, and a poor performance saw Wimbledon lose 2-1 and again out of every cup competition.

2011 was an historic year for AFC Wimbledon, but it had ended badly and things needed to change. So Brown acted. Minshull, Ademeno, James Mulley, Ryan Jackson and Porter were all slapped on the transfer list and told they would not play for the club again. Ademeno, who had his contract terminated soon after, and Porter, who moved to Newport County on loan once he recovered from injury, had only signed in the summer but had struggled to adapt.

New faces were required and defender Callum McNaughton, who had been on loan at the Dons for three months, was signed permanently from West Ham, who also loaned them midfielder George Moncur. Attacking midfielder Billy Knott came on loan from Sunderland and striker Byron Harrison was signed for a club-record fee from Stevenage that eclipsed the money spent on Main.

The final new arrival was an old face, as former Wimbledon FC striker Jason Euell signed on loan from Charlton Athletic. He had risen through Wimbledon's academy and made 141 appearances for them between 1995 and 2001, but his three-month stay at Kingsmeadow was disrupted by injury. He did bring some much-needed experience to the dressing room though.

The changes had an immediate impact, with Knott, Moncur, McNaughton, Euell and Harrison all starting in a 2-1 win at Port Vale that ended the horrendous run. It was followed by a remarkable 4-3 win at Gillingham, where Midson scored two late goals for victory and a 2-1 win over Macclesfield Town. It proved only a brief respite, as they took three points from their next seven matches to once more be looking over their shoulders at the relegation-threatened teams. A season-record 4,634-strong crowd saw them lose 2-1 at home to Aldershot, while Jolley scored his first goal in four months in the 3-3 draw at Crewe.

A crunch two weeks at the start of March would define Wimbledon's season. In the space of eleven days, they would face four teams below them in the table, three at home, and wins were vital to maintain their ten-point gap to the bottom two. The situation looked gloomy though, after 2-1 defeats at Hereford United and at home to Plymouth Argyle, who scored after just fourteen seconds. Uncharacteristically for Wimbledon fans, there were boos at the final whistle.

Brown and his players were under renewed pressure, particularly in defence. Brown had already dropped Stuart from the squad against Plymouth, but tore into the rest of his defenders after the match. He decided he had given them enough chances and brought in Brentford's Pim Balkestein on loan. The Dutchman gave Wimbledon exactly what they had been missing – a powerful, commanding centre-back. His made his debut against Dagenham & Redbridge and inspired the Dons to a 2-1 win through goals from Midson and Kieran Djilali, a winger signed earlier in the season but injured for most of it. That was followed by a 3-1 home win over Bradford, in which Midson scored two penalties and hit twenty goals for the season. There were ten games to go and Wimbledon were in a much healthier position as the gloom lifted.

Christian Jolley carries strike partner Jack Midson after scoring against Gillingham. The pair were rampant, scoring eight goals between them in four games. (Newsquest)

Former Wimbledon player Jason Euell arrived at AFC Wimbledon on loan from Charlton Athletic, but his stay was punctuated by injury. (Newsquest)

They continued to stumble their way through the League, but were never in any real danger of being caught up in a relegation battle. Harrison had struggled to find his best form but finally got off the mark in his thirteenth appearance, scoring an injury-time goal in a 4-0 home win over Burton, heading in on the goal line. Another striker with big expectations signed by the Dons was Jason Prior, who came from Isthmian Division One South Bognor Regis Town with an incredible record of sixty-six goals in just a season and a half. He was beset by bad luck though and, having missed two months with a knee injury, he suffered a horrific double leg break six minutes into his second competitive start at Crawley. Crawley's Hope Akpan was sent off for the challenge, but Prior faced nine months out. The match ended 1-1 with the point enough to guarantee Wimbledon's stay in the Football League with four games to go.

They finished with a flourish, thanks to a 3-1 home win over promoted Shrewsbury Town. Luke Moore's two goals took him into double figures for the season while Harrison got his second, again a tap in from a yard out. It was Stuart's farewell appearance, with the veteran already told his contract would not be renewed. He would be the first of many faces to leave AFC Wimbledon that summer.

They finished sixteenth, ten points clear of the bottom two, with Sammy Moore named supporters' player of the year, Radio WDON player of the year and Junior Dons player of the year. Billy Knott was given the young player trophy and Jack Midson the players' player of the year. Life in the Football League had been a baptism of fire and it was clear there was a lot of work to do if Wimbledon were going to consistently challenge at the correct end of the table next season.

13

A SAD GOODBYE AND OLD ENEMIES

Everyone knew changes were needed if AFC Wimbledon were going to be a force in the Football League. It meant some difficult decisions had to be made, and led to the emotional farewell of Terry Brown just eight games into the season. It ended what had been the perfect partnership between manager and club, but did instigate the return of another Wimbledon FC hero as his replacement. Among all the changes, there came one of the biggest and most controversial games in the Dons' history when the FA Cup once more threw up a potential tie against their fierce Milton Keynes rivals: this time it became a reality.

The first changes began in the week after the season ended as Brown culled his squad. Lee Minshull, Max Porter, James Mulley, Jamie Stuart and Ryan Jackson already knew they were heading out the door, but Gareth Gwillim, Chris Bush, Jack Turner, Fraser Franks, Brett Johnson, Reece Jones, Ricky Wellard, Kieran Djilali and Sam Hatton all joined them. Gwillim and Hatton were the most surprising, having played the majority of the previous season.

It left Brown with just eleven players, two of which were long-term injury victims Callum McNaughton and Jason Prior. Youngsters Jim Fenlon, Huw Johnson and Frankie Merrifield were all given professional contracts and Brown set about trying to find the right signings to push Wimbledon on. In came right-back Curtis Osano from Luton Town, nineteen-year-old midfielder Louis Harris from Wolves and experienced pair Stacy Long, a midfielder from Stevenage, and Warren Cummings, a left-back from Bournemouth who at thirty-one was Wimbledon's oldest player.

They were the only four signings by the time pre-season training kicked off, but they were soon joined by Pim Balkestein, who signed permanently from Brentford, and nineteen-year-old defender Angus MacDonald on a six-month loan from Reading, who beat the Dons 7-0 in their first friendly game.

There was also a friendly with a West Ham XI that ended in a 4-2 defeat. Before the game, there was a special testimonial match to celebrate Simon Bassey's ten years at the club that involved a host of AFC Wimbledon's playing heroes. Andy Little, Keith Ward, Matt Everard, Noel Frankum, Rob Ursell, Ryan Gray, Dave Fry, Simon Ray, Martin Randell, Joe Sheerin, Jon Main, Elliott Godfrey and Ben Thatcher (who had played for Wimbledon FC) all played, while Michael Haswell managed. Bassey's team won 4-3. The player-turned-coach even hit a hat-trick to complete the celebrations.

Just before the season started, Mikhael Jaimez-Ruiz came in as back-up goalkeeper to Seb Brown and striker Charlie Strutton was signed having done enough in pre-season to earn a deal.

The season once more started with a League Cup game and another cup fixture with Stevenage, following on from their FA Cup game two seasons ago and their Johnstone's Paint Trophy game last season. Cummings, MacDonald, Long and Balkestein made full debuts, while Harris came off the bench in a 3-1 defeat that included a Seb Brown blunder and Brendan Kiernan's first senior goal for the club. For the second season in a row though they had gone out at the first hurdle.

The new signings all talked up Wimbledon's promotion chances, and expectations were boosted by an opening-day 1-0 win over Chesterfield as Midson continued where he had left off last season with the only goal. Everyone hoped that would be the start of a season at the right end of the League, but it proved to be Terry Brown's final win at AFC Wimbledon.

Three days after beating Chesterfield, Wimbledon were thumped 6-2 at Burton Albion, where they were losing 4-0 after twenty-eight minutes, and followed that with a 5-1 defeat at Bradford. It had been a horrible few days and once more the fans were grumbling; so much so the Dons Trust board came out with a statement backing Brown after holding detailed discussions with the manager on what actions needed to be taken.

Brown had already signed one defender on loan, Curtis Haynes-Brown, and signed another two with Osano and Mat Mitchel-King missing through injury. George Francomb and Dale Bennett both played in a 2-2 draw at home to Dagenham & Redbridge, where Midson and Harrison scored and Seb Brown saved a penalty. That, however, was followed by a 2-0 defeat at Northampton and then two home games in four days against Rochdale and Torquay. It wasn't said publicly, but the feeling was that Terry Brown would leave if he lost both games. He delved into the transfer market once more and brought Steven Gregory back to the club on loan, as well as signing central defender Will Antwi.

Both started against Rochdale, when the new all-seater Kingston Road End stand was opened, but Midson was sent off in the first half for lashing out at Bobby Grant and the Dons slipped to a 2-1 defeat, with Luke Moore scoring a late consolation. There were four changes to the team against Torquay, but no matter what he did, Brown could not reverse Wimbledon's fortunes or their luck. Torquay won 1-0 with a calamitous goal, when Seb Brown's kicked clearance cannoned in off Rene Howe, and Christian Jolley was sent off late on for two bookings. It left Wimbledon perilously close to danger in twenty-first place.

With just four points from seven games, Terry Brown knew what was coming. At the end of the Torquay game he went around Kingsmeadow and completed an emotional, tear-filled lap of honour. The next morning, 19 September, it was announced that Brown and Stuart Cash were leaving by mutual consent after a remarkable five and a half years in charge. Brown had taken the Dons from the Isthmian League all the way to League Two, with three promotions in four seasons. But he had seemed out of his depth in League Two, with his biggest problem picking a settled side. In the seven League games and one cup game he had that season, he had used twenty-four different players.

It was a sad time for all at AFC Wimbledon and a difficult decision for the board to make, but Brown's place in the club's history is unlikely to ever be matched, and he would be seen at Wimbledon games many times throughout the rest of the season.

While the Dons searched for a new manager to follow in the footsteps of Terry Eames, Nicky English, Dave Anderson and Brown, Bassey was put in charge as caretaker and immediately made an impression. Sammy Moore's goal secured a vital 1-0 at Wycombe Wanderers, despite Harrison's penalty miss. That was followed by a 2-1 home defeat to Accrington Stanley and an unlucky 3-2 loss at Oxford, where the Dons hit the woodwork five times and Fenlon scored a 25-yard wonder goal. Harrison was hitting goalscoring form as well, and hit his fifth of the season in a 2-1 win over Plymouth Argyle that was Bassey's fourth and final match in charge.

His six points from four games and the noticeable improvement in performance had many calling for him to get the job full-time, and he did make the shortlist of three but missed out. Former Brentford manager Andy Scott was linked with the job after he was spotted at Terry Brown's final game in charge, and former Barnet manager and Wimbledon FA Cup hero Lawrie Sanchez was also in the running. But instead, it was another Wimbledon FC old boy who got the nod.

Neal Ardley made almost 250 appearances for Wimbledon between 1991 and 2002 and had been to watch the phoenix club many times since its formation, including their first home game against Chipstead in 2002. Eyebrows were raised at the decision, as Ardley had

Pim Balkestein cannot hide his disappointment after seeing a goal disallowed in the defeat to Rochdale that sent Terry Brown closer to the sack. (Newsquest)

Seb Brown picks the ball out of the net after his mistake gave Torquay United victory at Kingsmeadow and spelled the end of Terry Brown's time as manager. (Newsquest)

no experience of managing a senior team, but his record at bringing youth-team players through as Cardiff City's academy manager had swung the decision in his favour. Neil Cox was named as his assistant, with Bassey kept on as first-team coach. Despite his promises to take Wimbledon to the next level though, he would never quite manage to get them clear of safety until the very last day of the season.

He started with a 2-1 defeat at home to Cheltenham Town, former Don Kaid Mohamed scoring the winner, and then a 1-1 draw at Fleetwood when Harrison scored for the fourth game in a row. He got his first win in only his third game as Rashid Yussuff scored twice in a 3-1 win over struggling Bristol Rovers.

He only took four points from his next six games though, as he started to put his own stamp on the squad. Utility man Jonathan Meades was signed on loan from Bournemouth; Yado Mambo, who had been brought in from Charlton by Bassey, saw his loan extended; midfielder Jake Reeves came in on loan from Brentford; winger Djilali was re-signed and striker Paul McCallum came in on loan for a month, only to be sent off on his debut in a 3-1 defeat at Morecombe. Ardley also made the decision to replace his goalkeeper, bringing in his former Wimbledon teammate Neil Sullivan, now forty-two, on loan from Doncaster

Terry Brown, with tears in his eyes, takes a lap of honour around Kingsmeadow after the defeat to Torquay. He knew his time as manager would be up the next morning. (Newsquest)

Rovers. Sullivan had made 224 appearances for Wimbledon between 1988 and 2000 and took over from Seb Brown between the sticks. League results may have been taking time to come together as the new players gelled, but there were bigger fish to fry in the FA Cup.

The Dons were handed a first-round tie at York City and scraped a replay with a 1-1 draw thanks to Strutton's first Wimbledon goal. In the second-round draw the next day, they were once more handed the game they didn't want. In a repeat of two years ago, Wimbledon would meet MK Dons in the second round if they beat York in their replay and Milton Keynes beat Southern Premier Cambridge City in theirs after a 0-0 draw in their first game.

After the draw was made, Wimbledon made a similar statement to the one they made two years before:

> AFC Wimbledon is a fan-owned club. We are proud of that fact and also that we returned to the Football League the proper way, rising through the football pyramid. While we would rather not have been drawn in this tie, like everything we do, we will approach this game in a professional manner if it happens.

It did happen. Wimbledon won a thrilling replay with York 4-3 that included a Seb Brown own goal, York reduced to ten men after thirty-five minutes, Strutton scoring twice, York scoring a last-minute equaliser to force extra time and then goals from Harrison and Midson. A day later, MK beat Cambridge 6-1 and the grudge match became a reality.

There was talk of a boycott by Wimbledon fans not wanting to swell MK's coffers by going to the game at their stadium, but it never materialised. Fans that didn't want to buy a ticket though were allowed to donate the price of a ticket to Wimbledon instead.

The club itself kept the moral high ground, with Erik Samuelson handling all the extra media hype with his usual calmness. He admitted he would have rather had the game come after he had left, but talked eloquently of making sure they behaved themselves as a club and did not endanger the goodwill they had built up with the rest of football. He himself decided not to go to the game and instead went to the playground with his granddaughter. The rest of the board declined MK's hospitality and went as fans in the stand.

For the first time, MK chairman Peter Winkelman admitted the move to take Wimbledon to Milton Keynes in 2002 was wrong and that he was not proud of the way his club had come about. He did defend it as well though, saying the choice was either move the club or see it liquidated.

The build-up was ferocious, but finally the match itself came about on Sunday 2 December. Both sets of fans, Terry Brown included among the Wimbledon fans, behaved themselves. There were banners such as 'MK Scum' and a few chants, but the expected trouble never materialised and AFC Wimbledon's professionalism once more earned admirers. They did boo MK players David Martin and Dean Lewington, who had stayed with the club once it moved from Wimbledon, and cheered when a plane flew over the stadium trailing the banner 'We are Wimbledon'. MK fans for their part wore Wimbledon shirts from the 1990s and unfurled banners such as 'We are keeping the Dons – Get over it', in response to a campaign by the *Wimbledon Guardian* newspaper to get them to drop the Dons from their name.

On the pitch, MK were riding high in League One and expected to ease past the Dons, but Ardley's side put up a good fight and were unlucky to finish on the wrong end of a 2-1 scoreline. MK dominated the first half but Wimbledon, who gave Toby Ajala his first start on the wing after he signed on loan from Bristol City, held firm until the final minute when Stephen Gleeson struck a superb opener from distance.

Wimbledon improved after the break and equalised through Midson's header to spark wild celebrations with a few joyful fans spilling on to the pitch. They almost pulled off the win they craved when Gregory was put through on goal, but Martin got the slightest of touches to his low shot to push it just past the post. It was a miss he would regret in injury time when Jon Otsemobor's flick beat Sullivan and gave MK the win.

It was harsh on Wimbledon but they had done themselves justice and there was a small sense of relief the game had not gone to a replay back at Kingsmeadow. They earned £60,000 through gate receipts and were now able to concentrate on pulling away from the bottom of the League.

One fan shows off his feelings toward MK Dons as the two teams clash in the FA Cup at Stadium MK. (Paul Willatts)

Jack Midson dives to head home a cross to put Wimbledon level against their rivals and spark a mini pitch invasion from Dons fans. (Paul Willatts)

14

FIGHT FOR SURVIVAL

After the furore of the cup, AFC Wimbledon had to get back to their bread and butter in the League as Neal Ardley tried to steer them away from the relegation zone. Twice it looked like he had done just that, only for the Dons' form to dip twice more, and in the end it all came down to one miraculous, nerve-wracking Saturday afternoon on 27 April.

One point from three matches in December meant the Dons finished 2012 bottom of the entire Football League. It rammed home the severity of their situation, and left Ardley admitting a raft of new players were needed if they were to get out of the mess they were in. He also warned those already at the club that if they didn't change their mentality, they should leave.

In came midfielder Peter Sweeney from League One Bury and former fans' favourite Chris Hussey returned permanently, having been released by Coventry City after spending three years away from Kingsmeadow. Ajala, Sullivan and Meades saw their loans extended, but Steven Gregory and Yado Mambo left at the end of their stays and then chose to move to Gillingham and Shrewsbury over returns to the Dons. Christian Jolley was the biggest name to leave Kingsmeadow at the start of the month. Having spent time on loan at Newport County earlier in the season, he made the switch to Wales permanently having falling down the order under Ardley.

As well as a change in playing personnel, there was a change in results throughout January as the Dons went five games unbeaten. The only downside was seeing the other teams around them also pick up results to prevent Wimbledon moving clear.

There was a thrilling 3-2 victory at fellow strugglers Torquay United on New Year's Day thanks to Stacy Long's ninety-fourth-minute penalty after Torquay had equalised in the ninetieth minute. Paul McCallum then scored the winner in a 1-0 victory at Rochdale and hit the net twice more in a 2-2 draw with Wycombe Wanderers where Sweeney and Hussey made their debuts. There was even a 2-2 draw at home to League leaders Port Vale, where Jack Midson's double had given them a surprise 2-0 lead.

Ardley was not done rejigging his team and had a hectic final few days in the January transfer window. In came midfielder Harry Pell from Hereford United, defender Alan Bennett from Chesterfield and strikers Kevin Saint-Luce – after his release by Cardiff City – and thirty-three-year-old Gary Alexander, on loan from League One Crawley. He was the sixth signing of a manic window.

Going the other way were the fit-again Callum McNaughton, Kieran Djilali and Ryan Hervel – who didn't play for the first team despite being signed by Ardley two months earlier – who were all released. The biggest exit was Byron Harrison's. The striker, Wimbledon's record signing only twelve months previously, joined League Two rivals Cheltenham Town. After a good start to the campaign, scoring nine goals and topping the Dons scoring charts, he had missed a month with a back injury and was allowed to leave when the Robins came in for him.

The Surrey Senior Cup and London Senior Cup squads were once more filled with a blend of youth and first-team players in need of games, and neither competition brought silverware. There were wins against Ashford Town (Middlesex) (1-0 after extra time), Horley Town (4-1), and Chipstead (2-1) that put Wimbledon into the last four of the Surrey Cup, but there they were comprehensively beaten 5-2 by Sutton United. After a 4-2 penalty shoot-out win over Barking, Wimbledon were beaten in the quarter-finals of the London Cup when they went down 4-3 at Cray Wanderers.

The League was where it really mattered though, and Alexander made an instant impact with a goal in the 1-1 draw at home to Burton. But defeats to Port Vale (3-0) and Chesterfield (2-0) in a performance that had Ardley apologising to Dons fans, had everyone looking over their shoulders again.

It seemed their worries were premature, when a run of one defeat in eight matches seemingly ended all relegation troubles. Alexander's injury-time goal gave them a 2-1 win over play-off chasing Bradford, and Saint-Luce's 20-yard thunderbolt took the Dons off the bottom with a 1-0 win at Dagenham & Redbridge. There was a 1-1 draw with Plymouth and a 2-1 loss at Cheltenham, but three straight wins had some fans even dreaming of the play-offs.

John Sullivan came in on loan from Charlton to take Neil Sullivan's place in goal when the veteran was recalled by Doncaster, and made his debut in a vital 3-2 win over York City that included a second goal in four games for Brighton loanee Brennan Dickenson. Versatile defender Kelly Youga signed on a free, and made his debut in an emphatic 3-1 win at play-off hopefuls Southend United and then Midson's wonderful chip secured a 1-0 win over strugglers Aldershot.

After a 4-0 defeat at Accrington Stanley and 2-0 home win over Morecambe, with goals from Saint-Luce and Midson, the Dons sat sixteenth in the table, seven points clear of the bottom two with six games to play. They were only two points shy of the fifty-point mark Ardley had set for survival and a third season in the Football League beckoned.

No one could have predicted the drama that was to come, as three straight 1-0 defeats, coupled with wins for those around them, plunged them straight back into a fascinating relegation dogfight. The most damaging defeat of the three was at home to Barnet on Easter Monday as, despite dominating the game, they surrendered three valuable points to a relegation rival. With three games left, the Dons found themselves only two places and two points above the bottom two. It was difficult to pinpoint what had gone wrong but Ardley, like Brown before him, had struggled for a settled side. Since coming to the club in October he had signed seventeen players and played a staggering forty-one.

Luke Moore, the club's longest-serving player, stopped the losing streak by scoring twice in a 2-2 draw at home to Exeter that gave the record 4,749 crowd hope once more. But York won to go above them and Barnet, Torquay and Aldershot below them all had a game in hand. They played those games that week and Torquay beat Barnet to leapfrog

Brennan Dickenson stretches to score the second goal in a vital 3-2 win over relegation rivals York City that had Wimbledon moving away from the bottom two. (Newsquest)

Wimbledon. Now only Aldershot, four points behind them, and Barnet, one point behind them, were below the Dons.

In their penultimate game, Wimbledon faced the daunting prospect of getting a result at promoted Gillingham, who themselves needed a point to finish as champions. It appeared a forlorn task, when Deon Burton and AFC Wimbledon hero Danny Kedwell had Gillingham 2-0 up at half-time. The Dons never know when they are beaten though, and showed their fighting spirit after the break to claw back a deserved point. Midson and Meades got the goals for a 2-2 draw. It was a great point, but results elsewhere saw the Dons in the bottom two. Aldershot beat Dagenham & Redbridge to keep their hopes alive, and Barnet went above Wimbledon with victory over Wycombe. There were seven teams that could mathematically go down with one game left.

The maths was simple for Wimbledon. They hosted Fleetwood Town at Kingsmeadow, and knew a win would keep them up because York and Dagenham were playing each other and three points would definitely put the Dons ahead of one of them. A draw would have put them level on points with Barnet and Dagenham if they lost, but Wimbledon's poor goal difference would have seen them relegated.

Wimbledon's fight saw them in the media spotlight once more, but there was a belief they would do the impossible. Samuelson had said relegation would not be disastrous and that, no matter what, the club would still be theirs whatever division they were in. Ardley urged his players to stick to the script, and by the time 4,738 fans crowded into Kingsmeadow, there was a nervous excitement filling the stadium.

The Dons started at a fantastic tempo but couldn't find the breakthrough. Alexander had two shots saved, Pell was denied, Midson shot over the bar and Bennett had an effort cleared off the line all in the first half. Fleetwood were playing their part too, with Andy Mangan twice going close.

Midson hit the post and Pell had a shot cleared off the line before the Dons finally got the breakthrough on the hour mark. Sammy Moore floated in a free-kick, and Alexander escaped his marker to head home. Wimbledon, as it stood, were safe, and the fans were cheering enthusiastically. Their celebrations were such that, when Fleetwood drew level less than a minute later, many didn't notice until they saw Wimbledon kicking off. Mangan was the man to potentially send the Dons down, scrambling home a corner.

Wimbledon needed a hero to follow in the footsteps of Mark de Bolla in the 2008 Isthmian Premier League play-off final; Jon Main against Hampton & Richmond for the Conference South title in 2009; and Danny Kedwell against Luton in the Conference play-off final. That man was Midson. When Curtis Osano, making his first start since January, was felled in the box by Robert Atkinson, referee James Linington pointed to the spot. Midson took the ball and, with the whole of Kingsmeadow holding their breath, calmly sent Fleetwood's Scott Davies the wrong way. Once more, the Dons were staying up and Barnet, losing at Northampton, were going down.

Fleetwood pressed for an equaliser and Wimbledon just about repelled them. The final whistle went and the Dons had done it. The supporters invaded the pitch, and the players were lifted up on shoulders in celebrations that matched any from the many promotions.

Ardley admitted it would be difficult for anything in his managerial career to ever better the feeling and Midson, the WISA Allen Batsford player of the year who ended on fifteen goals, thanked the fans and revealed he had practised penalties after every training session during the season.

It was a special day for Wimbledon, but one they hope they won't ever have to repeat, as twelve years of history and promotions had come down to a final day relegation battle.

Luke Moore, Wimbledon's longest-serving player, celebrates scoring the first of two equalisers in the 2-2 draw with Exeter City that secured a massive point for the Dons. (Newsquest)

Gary Alexander, the third Wimbledon player from the right, watches as his header goes in off the post to put the Dons ahead against Fleetwood. (Newsquest)

But a minute after going ahead, Wimbledon concede an equaliser, and are once more facing relegation. (Newsquest)

Jack Midson punches the air after keeping his cool to put Wimbledon ahead from the penalty spot, a goal that kept them in the Football League. (Newsquest)

Goalscorers Midson and Gary Alexander share their delight with the Wimbledon crowd. (Newsquest)

15

NEW BEGINNINGS

AFC Wimbledon had done what they had always set out to do: regain their rightful place back in the Football League after it was stolen from them. It had been a miraculous journey from the muddy grounds and square goalposts of Sandhurst Town to the comparable delights of trips to Torquay United and Shrewsbury Town.

Players will always grab the headlines, and the likes of Kevin Cooper, Matt Everard, Richard Butler, Roscoe Dsane, Jason Goodliffe, Jon Main and Danny Kedwell have all earned their places in the history books. But things are different at Wimbledon, and the true heroes in south London are the fans that fought for their club when all seemed lost and are still there today.

Ivor Heller remains as commercial director, Kris Stewart is on the Dons Trust board and Erik Samuelson is still chief executive. Their dedication and that of Trevor Williams, Marc Jones and the hundreds of volunteers are what have made AFC Wimbledon the special club it is.

The summer of 2013 proposed a difficult question though. What next? If they are ever going to challenge higher up League Two and the Football League, does there need to be a change in mentality? If it means selling out, then no. Samuelson made it clear in the lead up to the relegation decider with Fleetwood that even if they did drop to the Conference, it didn't matter. What matters is the fans own their team, and that won't ever change.

In Neal Ardley, they also have a manager they feel can take them up a gear. He won't have millions to spend, but shrewd acquisitions like Harry Pell and Allan Bennett have already shown he has an eye for a player. His experience with youngsters at Cardiff City's academy will be vital too. AFC Wimbledon have built their own strong academy and a number of exciting prospects are expected to find their way into the first team under Ardley.

The ultimate goal will be to one day regain the second-tier status Wimbledon had in 2002 when the club was so unexpectantly ripped away from supporters. If they do that on the pitch, then to completely take back their history and identity there will only be one major outstanding issue left – their stadium and a return to Merton, something there had been developments on while they fought for their Football League status.

Wimbledon Greyhound track, next to Wimbledon's old Plough Lane stadium that has now been turned into flats, was in desperate need of redevelopment. In the summer of 2012, Wimbledon announced their hopes to build a 12,000-seater stadium there, responding to Merton Council's call for sites that invited businesses to submit ideas

Jack Midson gives the thumbs up after keeping AFC Wimbledon in the Football League. (Newsquest)

for new developments in the borough. The Dons faced competition though, as Irish businessman Paschal Taggart also put forward the idea of a new four-tier £30-million 6,000-seater greyhound stadium.

The Greyhound Racing Authority, which owns the greyhound stadium, backed Wimbledon by submitting proposals in October that welcomed the building of a 10,000-seater football stadium for the club to use. By February, the Dons submitted updated proposals of their ideas and Taggart did the same in March, changing his plans to a £60-million 4,500-seater greyhound stadium that would also include state-of-the-art squash courts, a supermarket and flats. In the summer of 2013, both proposals were with Merton Council with a decision on the preferred outcome, expected to be decided by the end of the year.

If the decision falls Wimbledon's way, then their miraculous journey from the dark day of 28 May 2002 will finally be complete.